Confessions of a Venture Capitalist

Confessions of a
VENTURE CAPITALIST

Inside the High-Stakes World of Start-up Financing

Ruthann Quindlen

WARNER BOOKS

A Time Warner Company

Warner Books, Inc., 1271 Avenue of the Americas, New York, NY 10020
Visit our Web site at www.twbookmark.com

(w) A Time Warner Company

Printed in the United States of America
First Printing: May 2000
10 9 8 7 6 5 4 3 2 1

Library of Congress Cataloging-in-Publication Data
Quindlen, Ruthann.
    Confessions of a venture capitalist : inside the high-stakes world of start-up financing /
Ruthann Quindlen.
        p.   cm.
    ISBN 0-446-52680-0
    1. Venture capital—United States. I. Title.
HG4963.Q35 2000
658.15'224—dc21

                                                                        99-049010

for David—

my favorite entrepreneur

and the "wind beneath my wings"

Acknowledgments

Thanks to:

My collaborator, Lisa Dickey, who did a great job and kept me sane throughout this whole process while putting up with my occasional moodiness. Ditto for my assistant Ann Doran.

The founders and CEOs of some of the actual or possible IVP investment companies, for supplying their advice and for letting me tell their stories in order to help other entrepreneurs. Particular thanks to David Hsieh of FaceTime Communications, who had the original idea for this book.

My partners, for giving me the opportunity to be a partner at IVP, for letting me write this book even though the concept was somewhat alien and scary to them, and for taking the time out of their busy schedules to review it.

My advisers—Abigail Johnson of Roeder Johnson, Seth Godin of Yahoo!, and Lisa DiMona of Lark Productions—without whom this book never would have happened.

My family—mother, brother, stepsons, and other relatives—who asked about how the book was going every weekend and thus kept me motivated.

Contents

Preface

Why Focus on Mistakes?

On reading the initial draft of this book, many people, including my editor, suggested that I add more Silicon Valley success stories to balance out those that focus on companies' mistakes. I chose not to do this. Not because there's any lack of successful companies—IVP is enjoying record returns these days—but because I believe it's difficult to learn much from success stories.

Usually, extremely successful entrepreneurs can't give a good answer to the question of why they were successful. They have a tendency to rewrite history, to forget all the missteps along the way, and to view the past as a straight line to success. Besides, most successful CEOs and founders are executives in public companies, so they're not exactly inclined to spell out their historical mistakes and missteps, which could affect the positive image of their company.

The most interesting thing about success is that it's often due mostly to a confluence of three factors: someone was in the right place, at the right time, with the right idea. That's a valuable thing for new entrepreneurs to know, but it's not the most effective and concrete lesson an entrepreneur can take away from a book like this.

Learning about mistakes is a different matter. In learning about mistakes others have made, a less seasoned entrepreneur can observe the likely results of certain decisions or actions. These are the stories that are truly valuable, and the lessons that are most effectively conveyed.

As a less seasoned venture capitalist, I was also learning during the time I wrote the book. That's something entrepreneurs should remember: We investors learn along the way too. Though we learn some different things than the entrepreneurs do, we're all aiming to avoid making common mistakes.

Risk versus Reward

A friend of mind from business school recently joined a start-up that's going through the venture funding process. When she remarked to me that venture funding dynamics are particularly inscrutable to new entrepreneurs, I explained that most decisions that investors make are fairly easy to decipher—it comes down to simply weighing risk and reward. If the potential opportunity is large enough, an investor will take on more risk. If not, more of the pieces of the puzzle have to be nailed down and in place.

This weighing applies to management teams, the maturity of the technology, the amount of money to be raised, the number of unanswered questions, the business models—to just about everything, really. As you analyze investors' actions in the following stories, that's a good thing to keep in mind.

Public Market Investing

When my editor asked me to include some advice on applying this book's lessons to public market investing, I was reluctant for a couple of reasons. First, the time frame for producing a book—from conception to writing to publishing—is a long one, and because things change so fast, it's best not to offer any specific recommendations on investing in any particular company. Also, it's best to seek suggestions on investing from professional stock market observers and equity analysts. So for those of you looking for a hot tip about the next Microsoft, you won't find it here.

What you will find, however, is something equally useful, if less specific. The lessons I describe in this book can be broadly applied to high-technology companies, both public and private. As with any investment, you should assess the market opportunity, the team, the business model, and the rest of the factors described in this book before investing. This information is widely available—from a company's initial public offering (IPO) prospectus, to reports by independent stock analysts, for example—both in print and online. These are the factors that will lead a high-technology company to success or failure, and you should understand them before taking a chance on a company's stock.

What's a Nice Girl Like Me Doing in a Place Like This?

Fifteen years ago, doing a public financing of a personal computer software company was almost as difficult as finding a nonstop flight from Baltimore to Silicon Valley. There was no interest in either. Both were destined to change.

August 1982 was the beginning of the longest and strongest bull market in history. That summer I was an intern at Alex. Brown and Sons, a Baltimore-based investment bank that later recruited me as a software analyst. I was still finishing up an MBA. None of us had any idea that this market would give unprecedented opportunity to entrepreneurs and investors. And we had even less of a clue about the impending revolution that would feed the bull market frenzy for years to come: the digitization of America. IBM had only a year earlier shipped its very first PC.

Alex. Brown and Sons was an odd place from which to participate in the digital revolution. Baltimore was a sleepy southern town far removed from Silicon Valley. The firm had been in the Brown family since its founding in the early 1800s, and much of the all-in-the-family, genteel old boys' culture remained. The place breathed old. The main room where the best brokers worked was canopied with an original

Tiffany glass dome that had been tarred over during World War II. Sunlight shone in around the cracks, and you always felt as if you were underwater in that room.

The firm's software corporate finance effort was led by Bev Wright, one of the first women partners on Wall Street. Bev was very tall, very smart, and very imposing. She always spoke in a whisper. I don't know whether she did it on purpose, but we all had to crane our heads forward to hear her in meetings, and through that technique she effectively controlled all discussion. Many of the executives from the largest mainframe software companies would not make a move without talking to Bev.

Many of the Alex. Brown brokers still sat at rolltop desks and still wore slicked-back hair, suspenders, and tiny wire-rim glasses. Beyond my official gray wool interview suit, which was of little use during a Baltimore summer, I had precious few clothes to wear in such a formal environment and no money to buy any. Somehow I managed to pull together a few jackets and skirts, along with some of those stupid floppy power ties that women wore in the 1980s, and I tried my best to fit in.

While cutting-edge Quotron monitors graced those rolltop desks, there was not a computer in sight. Who would have guessed that my summer project would be a step on the path to Alex. Brown's domination of equity financings for American software companies? And all without the help of computers!

By early 1983 the personal computer industry was exploding. Apple Computer had gone public. IBM was shipping the IBM PC in volume. Lotus Development launched the first spreadsheet, called 1-2-3, designed for the IBM PC, and reached $50 million in revenue its first year.

TIME magazine picked the personal computer as its Man of the Year for 1982 and ran a picture of a PC on its cover. I watched the Comdex computer trade show grow from a few hundred companies that year, displaying their wares on tables in a hotel room in Atlantic City, to taking Las Vegas captive the very next year with hundreds of thousands of visitors and miles of corporate booths.

When I graduated from Wharton I joined Alex. Brown full-time as Wall Street's first dedicated personal computer software analyst. Over the next ten years, the firm was to take public most of the leading personal computer software companies, including Microsoft, AOL, Aldus (PageMaker), Ashton-Tate (dBase), Borland (languages), Electronic Arts (games), and Broderbund (educational software). As either the research analyst or investment banker working with these companies, I helped attract the capital needed to accelerate the development of the PC software industry.

Meanwhile, the second major phase of the digital revolution was taking place—the growth of the nascent online and interactive media industries. In the mid-1980s, I had begun using an old character-based e-mail package from Lotus called Express, along with MCI Mail. These products were pretty primitive, but they allowed me to communicate with my entrepreneurs in a way my competition could not. It became clear to me that electronic mail and being online was a whole new experience and perhaps even a new industry.

My experience with America Online (AOL) really brought this home. When I first met with Steve Case, the founder and CEO of AOL, I thought the company was pretty interesting. By that time I had moved to California to work in Alex. Brown's West Coast office; since AOL was based in Virginia, I referred the company to one of my Baltimore partners. He, to my surprise, turned AOL down. When I heard this, I went to the mat for the company and resurrected the opportunity for Alex. Brown. In time I helped to convince my very skeptical partners that America Online was definitely an initial public offering (IPO) worth pursuing.

By 1993 I realized that I was sitting on the sidelines while yet another revolution was taking place. I wanted to move up the food chain and help to start companies, rather than just finance or follow them. I decided to become a venture capitalist. I also decided that rather than working with companies that already had revenues, which was very similar to my past experience, I would join an early-stage venture firm and focus on creating companies from the ground up. After talking to a few Silicon Valley partnerships, I decided to join Institutional Venture Partners (IVP), one of Silicon Valley's leading early-stage venture firms, as a partner focusing on software and interactive media.

My timing was perfect. America was evolving into an information economy, and technology was playing a larger and more significant role in the gross domestic product. Because of the strong stock market, capital was abundant—but great ideas and people were not. New technologies, such as the Internet, were radically changing both the face and the substance of computing. The telecommunications, computing, and consumer markets were beginning to overlap, producing even more new opportunities. Silicon Valley and venture capital were entering a golden age.

Early-stage venture capital investing is a roller coaster. It's thrilling to see a start-up flourish. But nothing takes the wind out of you more than watching a company you have invested in fail. Yet failure is a necessary component of venture capital; you embrace risk for appropriate return. You're trying to hit a home run, not merely to maintain a good batting average. One investment, if it is a real winner, can return the whole fund. This was a difficult concept for me—in fact, it took me four or five years to embrace.

The challenge of working on very early-stage companies was somewhat akin to a doctor moving from a specialty in pediatrics to one in obstetrics. The focus becomes forward-looking. As an analyst or investment banker, I usually began working with a company years in advance of any transaction. Nevertheless, the management teams were generally already in place, products were shipping, and the company had an established business model and some revenue.

Although I worked with many venture capitalists while an investment banker, I never really understood much about their daily life or motivations. In particular, I was always amazed at how anxious they appeared when it came time to take one of their companies public. Any little setback, any little delay—common occurrences when dealing with Wall Street or the Securities and Exchange Commission (SEC)—drove them into a frenzy. While I knew their companies' initial public offerings (IPOs) were important to them, I never really appreciated or understood their level of anxiety. Then, when I became an early-stage venture investor, it all became very clear.

An investor on the eve of an IPO is like a proud parent watching his or her child about to graduate from college: years of effort are concentrated into a single event. Watching your "child" mount the podium leads to reflection on the pain and heartache that went into getting there—getting financing, watching the team mature, overcoming obstacles.

And like parents, we venture capitalists worry that something could go wrong at the last second—a lawsuit out of nowhere, some change in the company's fortunes, the resignation of the CEO or a key manager— and derail the big event. In this era of Internet IPOs, where the time from founding to IPO has shrunk from five years to two to three, or even less, this anxiety level has been mitigated somewhat. But even with shortened time periods and an easier financing environment, some nervousness remains.

This, in a nutshell, is the key difference between being an investor and being an analyst or an investment banker for a company. The old adage about the hen and the pig providing a breakfast (of ham and eggs)—the hen is "involved," but the pig is "committed"—is the perfect analogy. The analyst/banker is "involved," but the investor is "committed." Emotionally, the risk is much greater—but so are the rewards.

As difficult and draining as working in venture capital can be, I really do enjoy it—and sometimes never more than when a company passes through a hard time and emerges successful. I never had children of my own (and my stepsons were adults when I remarried), so I was never personally privileged to experience a parent's relief and joy at watching from the audience as a beloved child graduated from college. But having been an investor in early-stage companies, I can certainly appreciate the emotions.

I made the transition from investment banker to venture capitalist because I came to believe that the more critical elements in defining a company's future success are established at its more formative early stage. Business models and marketing strategies are defined, management teams are built, product direction is established, competition is identified, and the whole corporate culture is set.

I have since learned that there are a finite number of things that can go right in helping an entrepreneur start a company and guide it to producing reasonable revenue, but no end to the number of things that can go wrong. In fact, most companies never make it to the public offering stage—they generally fail or have to be sold long before that happy event. Despite the higher risk, I still prefer to invest in very early-stage companies, called "raw start-ups." I like helping an entrepreneur, usually a technical founder, to define a strategy, a business model, a product, and a market; to attract other investors; and to recruit a management team. An entrepreneur might make very similar mistakes when the company is just starting its existence or when it's just finishing its IPO—but the difference is, mistakes in the start-up phase can be fatal.

That recognition was the genesis for this book. I have two goals in writing it. One is to help entrepreneurs bypass some of the common mistakes that I have observed when they start and build a company, whether they plan to interact with Wall Street or not. The second is to help mainstream America understand more about the venture capital economy—and the magic that is Silicon Valley.

Life in the

Bubble

Chapter 1

Working in the Bubble

I referred to the magic of Silicon Valley. That magic—an intoxicating mix of money, imagination, and inspiration—had its origin in the semiconductor boom of the 1970s, when dozens of companies seized on possibilities made ripe by Intel's development of the first microprocessor. Millions of dollars were generated, new industries were born, and a hilly strip of land south of San Francisco, land that was once home to a sprawling patchwork of orchard groves, became popularly known as "Silicon Valley."

Today Silicon Valley feels like a bubble. I should know: We venture capitalists live, work, eat, drink, and schmooze right smack in the center of that bubble. And so do most of the entrepreneurs.

The word "bubble" conjures different images for different people. Some may think of soap bubbles—translucent and beautiful, but fragile and short-lived. Others may think of the rich and famous, always caught in the fishbowl, or even of closed-environment bubbles like Biosphere II, where people try to recycle air and live off of their own waste products.

Silicon Valley is something like all of these bubbles. It is an enclosed, wealthy, fragile yet beautiful, breathing-its-own-fumes kind of place. And it is no exaggeration to say that there is no other place on earth quite like it.

There is a kind of bull's-eye target effect at work in the geography of Silicon Valley. Entrepreneurs live and work in towns and developments ranging all the way from San Francisco down the Pacific coast to Monterey. Venture capitalists, the keepers of the capital that fuels the Valley, generally live within a twenty-mile radius stretching out from Stanford. But the financial ground zero of Silicon Valley is a single street, the one street where almost all the venture capitalists work: Sand Hill Road in Menlo Park.

Sand Hill Road, which lies on land owned by Stanford University, runs close by the idyllic, palm-tree-lined Stanford campus. A wholly unremarkable road lined with low-slung buildings, gently sloping hills, and scrub brush, it begins with a riding stable and Christmas tree farm on the west side of Interstate 280 and runs for about three miles east before ending unceremoniously in the parking lot of the Stanford Shopping Center.

It's difficult to picture tycoons of finance and technology making deals in such a tranquil-looking setting. But dozens of venture capital firms line this street, representing some of the most powerful investors in one of the most influential businesses in the country. Some of the firms on Sand Hill Road—firms like Kleiner Perkins, Mayfield, Sequoia, and IVP—have name recognition of their own. Even better known are the names of companies that Sand Hill Road venture capitalist have invested in: Sun Microsystems, Netscape, Cisco, Intel, Apple, Excite, Yahoo! These companies are changing the way the world computes and communicates, and many got their start with assistance from Sand Hill Road venture capital firms. In any given year, the venture capitalists on this stretch of road might collectively represent as much as $10 billion worth of investable capital.

The mere words "Sand Hill" now hold an almost mystical meaning within Silicon Valley. The road has taken on a persona of its own: in the Valley you will hear people say, "Sand Hill thinks like this," or "Sand Hill didn't go for that idea." Being part of the so-called Sand Hill crowd, you can sometimes forget that the rest of the country—not to mention the world—may not be in on the reference.

I was once asked to address the leaders of the National Association of Broadcasters at Pebble Beach in Carmel Valley—a mere hundred miles from Silicon Valley. The title of my speech was "A View from Sand Hill." Trouble was, nobody knew what I was talking about. I spent the first ten minutes of my one-hour talk explaining the concept to them, which was a new experience for me. Explain what Sand Hill Road is? I had been living in the bubble so long that it hadn't occurred to me that people outside it might not know what I was talking about.

Silicon Valley is a place for people with ideas. It is a place where the right idea at the right time can yield remarkable returns for investors and entrepreneurs. It is known, rightly, as a place of simmering, sometimes spouting, creative enterprise.

How ironic, then, that the venture capitalists who nurture this creativity aren't more creative in their choices of where to meet, eat, and mingle. The best example of this is the phenomenon of the Silicon Valley breakfast. Breakfast is a prime time here for discussing potential deals. Everyone—and I really mean everyone—in Silicon Valley goes to one of three restaurants to do this: Buck's in Woodside, Il Fornaio in the heart of Palo Alto, and Hobee's in the Town and Country Shopping Center in Palo Alto. Same restaurants, same faces, everyone sitting within earshot of each other, bolting coffee and interviewing entrepreneurs.

Take Buck's, for example. It's your basic family-style eatery, with brown leather booth seats and green Formica tabletops. The walls and floors are covered with kitsch—cowboy boots, giant stone turtles, dinosaur models—and the last time I was there, there was a glass case on the counter displaying the latest book on Silicon Valley by long-ago Apple evangelist Guy Kawasaki. The menu is your basic breakfast fare (the pancakes are great; I get them every time), save for the occasional item, like the nonfat organic omelette, that indicates you're in California.

All kinds of people come to Buck's—entrepreneurs, parents with kids, graduate students from Stanford, guys in pickup trucks. (Of course, Buck's is in the upscale suburb of Woodside, which means that the pickup trucks are fancy, freshly painted, and driven by people who own horses and lots of land.) And lots and lots of venture capitalists and entrepreneurs.

Think about this behavior for a moment. Venture capital feels like one of the most competitive businesses on earth: at the extreme, it is a lot of money chasing a few good deals. Yet we venture capitalists and entrepreneurs stick together like a roving band, working and eating at the same places, staying in one another's orbit. Many times I have sat in one of the brown leather booths at Buck's and overheard things that I should not have heard—about corporate mergers, or the potential firing of an executive, or just some juicy gossip—all the while munching away on my pancakes.

What is it that makes us all want to be so much together? I've got my own theory. Venture capital is hard. It's stressful. It's lonely. Decisions that you help to make may lead to millions of dollars of loss or profit for your firm—to say nothing of the lives of people whose jobs partially depend on what you decide. In such an out-on-the-edge environment, where at any given point in time you are always wrong about something, it probably just feels better to be with other colleagues in a similar situation.

The managers of the companies that we fund marvel at this herding behavior. But in their favor, the venture capitalists' proximity to one another makes the entrepreneur's job of raising money easier. An entrepreneur can schedule numerous meetings—sometimes up to four in a row—for one day, and just zip up and down Sand Hill Road to get to them. I can't tell you how often entrepreneurs make sure to drop hints that they're seeing other venture capitalists. They announce breathlessly that they can't stay long because they're scheduled for a meeting just down the road, or they apologize for arriving late because they're coming from a meeting just up the road.

Sometimes we invest like a herd too. A notion will sweep Sand Hill that a certain type of company is hot, and five or six of these companies will suddenly materialize and come knocking on our doors within a single month. They will more than likely all get investments—after all, nobody wants to get left out of the Next Big Thing (which you'll read about at greater length in another chapter),

But this herdlike investing is inherently dangerous, sometimes resulting in whole categories of companies with markets that never quite take off. Consider, for example, Internet "push" companies, which were supposed to change the way we got information online by delivering information directly so the customer didn't have to spend time searching it out. This market soared on momentum as excited venture capitalists pumped money into it. The venture herd surged forth, and lots of companies got lots of money. By the mid-1990s, more than thirty "push" companies had reportedly been started. But hype, momentum, and the herd mentality do not guarantee success in a market. After about eighteen months the momentum fueling the "push" phenomenon fizzled.

One more defining characteristic of life in the bubble is the astonishing degree to which everyone—and I really do mean everyone—is tuned in, wired, or tied in to the communications revolution going on. Cleaning ladies carry cell phones. High schoolers carry pagers. People stand in line at the grocery store and debate the merits of Yahoo! versus other Internet search engines. In Silicon Valley, the threshold of awareness of the latest industry innovations and trends is exponentially higher than in the rest of the country.

This is one of the key ingredients of the magic I mentioned earlier: Silicon Valley is a place where the extraordinary is ordinary. It is a place where things not yet seen or dreamed of by most of America are already commonplace—or even outdated. It is an atmosphere in which entrepreneurs, investors, and inventors push one another to ever higher peaks of creativity.

But as remarkable as this atmosphere might be, it has been fueled even more by the sudden emergence of an exciting new technology: the Internet.

Chapter 2

The Internet Explosion

Many years from now, when historians look back on the late twentieth century, they will see the development of the commercial Internet as a clear dividing line. Life before the 1990s will be known as "B.I."—a seemingly ancient and virtually unimaginable time before the Internet became a part of everyday life. Already there is a generation of Americans old enough to use the Net and too young to remember that there was ever life without it.

The curious thing about this is that the Internet has actually been around for decades. Long before Yahoo! became a household name, the Internet—then known as ARPANET—was the primary communications medium among universities and government research labs. We have cold war paranoia to thank for the Internet: it was invented as a way to ensure that essential government data wouldn't be lost in the event of nuclear catastrophe. Even if a nerve center like Washington or New York were destroyed, went the theory, the country's vital information would still exist in the network, unscathed by the physical destruction of certain key computers.

I wish I could say that all of us technology tycoons and venture capitalists in Silicon Valley were prescient enough to recognize what the impact of the Internet would be from the very beginning, but we were not. For years—decades, even—no one was. It took a new breed of entrepreneur, one not blinded by the past, to take advantage of this phenomenon.

The wave started slowly. The Internet had been practically unusable for the masses until the creation of the World Wide Web, a system that suddenly bestowed relative order on the chaotic sprawl of information located in the growing computer network. Then a team of students at the University of Illinois, led by a baby-faced programmer named Marc Andreessen, created the tool that would forever change how ordinary people use their computers: the browser.

The development of the browser, though no one grasped it just yet, was a watershed event, one that would effect tremendous economic, as well as social, impact. With his new magical tool, Andreessen, who was still in his early twenties, took his team and a small investment from Jim Clark, a founder of Silicon Graphics, and in 1994 started a company called Netscape.

At the time, I don't think that any venture capitalists realized what a whole new ball game investing was about to become. The price for the investment in Netscape—$40 million before any money from venture investors went in—seemed high. I mean, here was a new company, founded by students using knowledge from a university project, with a product they were *giving away*—and they received a $40 million valuation. By historical venture capital standards, it appeared risky. But the Net was to bring profound changes in investors' thinking about founders, business models, required capital, and potential return.

Little did any of us know it, but just one year later Netscape would be worth several billion dollars. In an event that's already gone down in Internet industry lore, Netscape's stock doubled on the day of its initial public offering in August 1995, and by day's end the company was worth $2.1 billion. Don't get me wrong: we knew this Internet thing was going to be big. But how could we have known it would be this big?

In the summer of 1994, just after Netscape received funding, IVP funded a small start-up called Architext. The company basically consisted of a few Stanford students with an information-searching technology; we helped them apply that technology to searching out sites on the Internet. Yahoo!, another search-oriented company, had been founded about a year before, also by a group of Stanford students.

At the time, we toyed with the idea of putting these two start-ups together rather than having two small competitors. Neither company wanted to pursue that path, as each was convinced something far bigger lay in its own future. We all know what happened with Yahoo!—it became the Internet wunderkind company, worth tens of billions of dollars within a matter of years. And Architext? Just over a year later it became Excite; it grew to become the number two search company, and in 1999 it was bought by cable modem company @Home for $6.7 billion. One has to wonder what kind of powerhouse the early union of Yahoo! and Excite might have wrought.

After the summer of 1994, the deluge began: potential Net investments poured in at a faster and faster clip. With the release of the browser, more and more people began turning to the World Wide Web; suddenly the nascent Internet industry began to resemble the great California gold rush. Dozens of new Internet companies were being formed and funded daily, ideas became the currency of Silicon Valley, and the hype grew. Everyone wanted a piece of the action.

IVP leaped aggressively into Net investing. We had technology people from companies like Sun Microsystems come in and talk to us about the new industry. As early as the winter of 1993–94, we believed that the Internet would matter. What we didn't fully comprehend was that it would affect all facets of life: social, entertainment, business, infrastructure—everything.

IVP had two partners working on Net investments at the time: Geoff Yang and me. Geoff, who has a Stanford MBA and is a consummate athlete (he played on the Princeton tennis team and is a good golfer as well), is one of those guys whose life is defined by the deft touch of success. By January 1995, early in Internet time, IVP had made three consumer-oriented Net investments: in Excite, Mpath (later renamed HearMe), and GolfWeb.

While it was clear at the time that the Net was big and going to get bigger, the business models on the Net were still highly unproven. The early stumbling block was the "free" ethic that reigned on the Net. No one using the Web wanted to pay for anything; advertising supported the sites. Software and tools were given away. It seemed a breach of "Netiquette" to charge for anything.

This tactic—the giving away of a company's primary product—was unprecedented in the American business landscape. It was an outgrowth of the unusual distribution model made possible by the Internet. For the first time, companies could offer to deliver a product that required no middleman, and therefore none of the costs associated with a middleman, because users could simply download software over their modems. While it might seem odd to give away one's product—where would the revenue come from, after all?—there was a plan behind it.

Companies like Netscape who gave away their product were operating under a few certain principles. First, they realized that since the product and the ideas behind it were so new, they weren't likely to reach a large number of consumers if they charged for it. Better, they reasoned, to give the product away, get people used to using it, and then charge for upgrades. Also, corporate customers frequently purchased site licenses for the product, which put some money into the Net companies' coffers.

In 1999 this idea has morphed again: now there are Web companies devoted to selling goods at—or even *below*—cost, with the difference made up by ads on the Web site or other partnership arrangements. Buy.com is the most visible of these companies; though it's too soon to tell how they will fare, the idea behind them is at least theoretically plausible. But regardless of the sound reasons behind this "free" ethic, to a businessperson accustomed to aiming for profit, the idea of a company giving away its product seemed radical.

In fact, this was what kept software behemoth Microsoft from being an early Net player. Bill Gates, an archcapitalist, used to complain of this get-it-free mentality regularly. How could he make any money, after all, by offering all of his software for free? As a result of his reluctance to accept this new kind of business model, Bill almost missed the initial wave of the Internet frenzy.

I remember talking to Bill about the Internet at a dinner in the fall of 1994. We were in Phoenix, Arizona, at the Agenda computer industry conference, one of those invitation-only, movers-and-shakers conferences that dot the calendars of company executives.

At the time, Microsoft was putting serious money and effort behind Microsoft Network (MSN), a proprietary online service intended to compete with America Online (AOL). Microsoft was pouring money into MSN, which at the time was focused on developing original, proprietary content rather than simply linking to all the free content that already existed on the Web. Uncharacteristically for him, Bill was slow to grasp that by neglecting the Web, Microsoft was investing in the past rather than the future.

It was as if Silicon Valley had a powerful secret, one that for once was not being dominated out of the gate by Microsoft. The secret: The Web was going to change everything about the way we communicate, learn, shop, and entertain ourselves. It was poised to become the fastest-growing, most freewheeling industry the country had seen in decades. And it would gain strength from the diversity of small companies and erratic inventors who nurtured it. What it didn't need was a few big companies trying to dominate and shape it.

Others felt this way too. At the Agenda dinner, a casual first-night affair where the most powerful CEOs in the PC business munch tacos and pasta while wearing blue jeans and name tags, we all mingled outdoors, sweating in the sweltering Arizona night air. I was chatting with Bill, in one of those rare moments when he wasn't surrounded by people, and telling him about a new investment of mine—an Internet company whose service would enable online multi-player games.

Bill was asking questions and discussing the opportunities for such technology on MSN, when Philippe Kahn, the founder of Borland, stepped up to listen in. After a while, Bill's attention was drawn elsewhere, and Philippe took the opportunity to pull me to one side. Out of Bill's earshot, he warned me off conveying any more information. The reason? "You don't want him to know too much," Philippe said. I knew instantly what Philippe meant. Bill is brilliant. But it was weird to think that the rest of us were intrigued by something—the Internet—that Microsoft might not dominate.

Rob Glaser, a former Microsoft executive, was in on the secret. In early 1994 he founded a company called Progressive Networks, with primary funding from Mitch Kapor, the founder of Lotus Development. Progressive later morphed into Real Networks, an audio-video streaming company that eventually came to be worth billions of dollars. Real Networks filled a niche in the burgeoning Internet industry by setting the standard for multimedia on the Web.

I remember having fierce arguments with Rob, who's a very tenacious guy, like a bulldog who gets a bone in his teeth and won't let it go. This was in 1995: I was afraid that Microsoft would kill the Web when they gave MSN away for free with their Windows operating system. I feared that if all users of Windows—which by then was nearly everyone buying new computers—ended up signing on to MSN and using its proprietary content, interest in the Web would wane, and it might simply wither away. The idea seems quaint now, but at the time few foresaw the way the Web would explode. But Rob did: he assured me that the Internet was a much bigger phenomenon than Microsoft. He was, of course, right.

By 1995 and '96, more people got in on the secret, which was becoming less and less secret every day. Paul Allen, who cofounded Microsoft with Bill Gates, had seen the possibilities of the Internet as early as 1992. He founded Starwave, an Internet sports site aligned with ESPN, way ahead of most other destination sites. His investment was shrewd: Disney later acquired Starwave for $400 million.

The Internet changed the world of technology—and of venture capital—dramatically. Everything suddenly speeded up by an order of magnitude. Product cycles went from eighteen months to six months and later to three months. Hype over the Net's potential meant companies could go public after only one year, even when they were still losing money. IPOs for tiny, year-old companies made kids just out of college instant millionaires, and start-ups were suddenly worth billions, skewing the returns of the venture capital firms that invested in them. It was as though a long-pent-up animal had been unleashed.

Chapter 3

VC Does Not Stand for Viet Cong

I was discussing what it means to be a venture capitalist not long ago with a fairly new one—a former marketing executive who had recently joined a leading venture firm. He and I agreed that there was no other job like it.

"It's amazing," he said, "how many important decisions we help entrepreneurs make each day. And we get to invest millions in a single decision." What really struck him was the contrast between the kind of serial, frenzied, and near-constant big-decision-making a venture capitalist does and the demands of his former life as an executive in a technology company, where decisions that could make or break the company were comparatively few and far between.

I agreed with him. Life as a venture capitalist is unique, though not necessarily in ways you might think. Though the very term "venture capitalist" conjures some exotic vision of high-rolling, high-flying adventurism, the truth is actually pretty different. In my pre-venture days, when I was an analyst and then an investment banker, I had to be prepared to jet all over the world at a moment's notice. Once, for example, I flew to London for lunch and then back home to San Francisco in a single day. And once, when I was working on a Nippon Steel corporate investment in Oracle Corporation, I took a one-day round trip to Tokyo. I felt like I returned before I had even left. Considering my back-and-forth crossing of the international date line, maybe I had.

But life as a venture capitalist is much more rooted in the bubble of Silicon Valley. We rarely travel except to attend conferences or give a speech. Most of our portfolio companies—those on whose boards of directors we sit—are located within the Bay Area. The IVP office is located on Sand Hill Road, probably a total distance of about four miles from my front door. Although the days are often long, starting with an early breakfast and ending with late dinner, the fact that travel is limited primarily to the Bay Area takes the sting out of a twelve- or fourteen-hour day.

Although the life of a venture capitalist is not exactly a glamorous one, some partners have achieved a degree of fame through their success: John Doerr of Kleiner Perkins is the obvious example. He's achieved a kind of rock-star visibility within Silicon Valley.

John is a whippet-thin, intense person who fairly vibrates with energy. It's no wonder he's so thin, as he's the kind of guy who seems always to be in motion, even when he's standing still. To most of the world, he's an iconic, incredibly successful venture capitalist. But I know him as a great father to his two daughters, a good friend, and a fearless adventurer. And he's the best salesman I ever met. On any decision needing persuasion, John's usually the winner. The other person ends up doing something they never intended to—and still liking John nonetheless.

Although you may have only heard about this profession in recent years, venture capital has actually been around for quite a while. In the 1940s, venture firms, such as Venrock and J. H. Whitney, were formed to invest private fortunes—for example, the Rockefeller fortune. This type of investing was viewed as a patriotic activity, especially since many technology centers in the Northeast that received funding were critical to national defense. The 1950s and '60s brought the forerunners of today's professionally managed venture partnerships.

IVP was founded by one of the lions of the venture industry, Reid Dennis, who started its predecessor company (called IVA) in the early 1970s. At the time, IVA was the only fund in the United States of more than $10 million, and it represented 45 percent of all of the money raised by private partnerships. Reid is a consummate venture capitalist. Even before venture investing became an industry, Reid, who used to work for American Express, would listen to entrepreneurs' presentations over lunch and fund them out of his own pocket. So founding his own venture firm was a natural step.

The firm has ten general partners, seven of whom focus on technology (for example, Internet companies) and three of whom focus on life sciences (for example, medical products). We invest primarily in the earliest stages of a company's existence. Not only do we help new companies recruit executives, we also have offices at IVP where they can work—sort of a "company incubator" here in our building. Our investments have ranged from $100,000 to $5 million.

The IVP offices are Northern California corporate chic—light blond wood office furnishings, a high, peaked ceiling with skylights, green (for money) overtones. Our office is filled with Reid's art and rare collectibles, including an assortment of scale-model steam engines, sailing ships, and train cars displayed in glass cases throughout the building, and a collection of nineteenth-century lithographs and drawings of San Francisco.

Apart from "The Earthquake Room"—a conference room decorated with photographs of San Francisco in ruins after the 1906 earthquake—our conference rooms are named for the companies that have produced some of our greatest returns: Excite, Clarify, and Seagate. The criterion for having a conference room named after a company is this: Our portion of the investment at the time the stock is to be distributed must be worth $100 million. We challenge our newest companies to achieve this goal, and they in turn all tell us we're going to have to build more conference rooms (something we'd happily do, of course!). I keep my fingers crossed that more than one of my companies will be represented one day.

Venture capitalists invest money provided by limited partners into start-up companies. The venture capital fund prefers limited partners—such as university endowments or pension funds—that represent a long-term, consistent source of money. Typically, personal investors are not invited to invest in a venture capital fund because of the up-and-down nature of the industry.

For the money and assistance that we provide a company, we generally get a position on the board (which represents a bit more involvement than companies might get from some other forms of investing) and a percentage of equity. We also work closely with the founders, getting involved in helping to hire teams or planning a strategy.

Our goal is simple: to help the entrepreneur build a great company. Success is measured by the company's being able to (a) go public or (b) sell to another company for a high price. Once that happens, we take the money made and distribute it back to the limited partners in the form of stock or cash, giving them back the capital they invested plus a return. Putting money into a venture capital fund is a much riskier investment than putting money in the stock market, but the returns can be much, much greater.

The trick is to fund the companies that will become great companies and yield the highest returns. This, of course, is easier said than done—especially considering how few investments we are able to fund from the many great-sounding ideas we're presented. I'd say that for every company IVP decides to fund, we have probably heard several hundred proposals. Granted, we do fund fewer proposals because we get involved with companies at the earliest stage, when they'll require more of our time, but still, the numbers speak volumes.

The compensation for a venture capitalist is great (if you're successful, that is), the work is fascinating, and the schedule is much less physically demanding than that of many start-up executives. So what makes this life so challenging?

I found out quickly enough after joining IVP: It's the decisions you have to make, all day, every day. These decisions may mean life or death for the companies in which your firm has invested; they are sometimes hard, wrenching decisions to make. Should you recommend that the board hire or fire a CEO? Should your firm invest millions of dollars more in a failing enterprise, or give up and write the whole thing off? Generally, management and investors make these difficult decisions together, but that does not make them any easier.

Here's a typical afternoon for a venture capitalist: An aspiring founder comes in to pitch his company. The person pitching the idea is someone whose life is completely and utterly intertwined with his dreams for the company. He's coming in to give you everything he's got in the hour that you have allotted him, in the hope that you'll grant his wish: to help him create a great company. This help takes several forms, only one of which is money. Yes, entrepreneurs are looking for money from venture capitalists, but they're also seeking assistance, advice, and the benefit of our experience in building companies. And in building a great company, having a good partner is more important than simply having money.

Perhaps you like the founder's pitch. It's a good idea, and the founder seems to have a workable vision for the company. You are interested—but you also have heard pitches from two other companies that are equally interesting. You can't pursue all three, so which do you choose? And which do you drop? And what if the companies that you drop end up being the ones that set the industry afire—and the one you pick ends up fizzling?

I have never had another job where the capacity to second-guess your own decisions is so pervasive. And what's more, the feedback loop is incredibly long. It's a prolonged nerve-racking process to make a company. For all the work you do in helping to fund and work with a new company, you may not know whether you made a good investment until, say, five years or so have passed, and the company blossoms—or dies.

After I started working at IVP, I began suffering from insomnia in the early-morning hours. From about 2 A.M. to 6 A.M. every morning I found it impossible to sleep. I was always thinking about this company or that deal, and I began to worry that perhaps I wasn't cut out for this kind of work.

Then I had a memorable conversation with two other women venture capitalists at a golf clinic. "I'm having trouble sleeping," I told them. "I wake up at two A.M. and can't get back to sleep. Do you ever have insomnia?" The women looked at me incredulously, and one of them replied, "You're able to sleep until two?" I guess I was one of the lucky ones. Another very successful male venture capitalist classified his investments into "ones you can make and sleep" and "ones you cannot." He tries to balance these into a diversified portfolio of sleep deprivation.

There is another fascinating—and frightening—element of venture capital that has emerged in the last ten years. The stakes, which were high to begin with, have gone up exponentially.

In the early 1970s there were at most seven or eight venture capital firms, almost all of which were located in Silicon Valley. These firms invested in a few select technology areas, such as computer systems, disk drives, or other types of computer-related hardware.

Venture capital was a gentleman's club of understanding at that time; most partners belonged to the same clubs, lived in the same locations, and sent their children to the same schools. They formed syndicates of firms to invest in a single common deal, thus alleviating the risk for each firm. Things are different today. Firms are competitors rather than collaborators, thanks to the large sums of money that each venture firm must now invest.

Today there is less time and less collaboration, but more money, competition, and areas in which to invest. In the 1970s, venture investors were focused on investments in semiconductors and computers;

now we invest in everything from content on the Net to optical technology. And the excesses of the 1990s stock markets have made money itself a commodity. IVP's most recent fund, raised in early 1998, was $350 million—and it was not the largest fund by any means. By comparison, IVP's first fund in 1980 had $22 million to invest, and was one of the larger funds at that time.

There are now hundreds of venture capital firms, stretching from California to Boston. New firms are created every day. Companies are successful if they create billion-dollar market capitalizations in the stock market—and sometimes this takes only a few years. The velocity of change, growth, and opportunity has accelerated dramatically, and the notion of "success" has similarly been redefined.

I am reminded of an old adage: "Success has many fathers, but failure is an orphan." That perfectly sums up being a venture capitalist. Your partners will give you advice and support for difficult decisions and particularly for your mistakes and failures, but I believe that the mistakes and failures are really yours to live with in the long run.

And making mistakes is a given. As I mentioned earlier, the upside opportunity in my situation is limited, but the number of things that can go wrong with a start-up company is not. From misjudging the potential in a seemingly hot new market to helping to hire the wrong executives—any number of things can thwart an investment. And there is no way to learn incrementally: there are not enough funding opportunities in a lifetime to make all the possible mistakes and learn from them.

But the one thing to remember—and this goes for entrepreneurs as well as for venture capitalists—is that even though there are typically many moderate successes for every home run, that one whopping success is enough to make up for the rest, from both a psychological and an economic standpoint. After all, the best sluggers in baseball also frequently lead their teammates in strikeouts. But it's the home run they're going for, and sometimes it's only a home run that can make the difference.

Chapter 4

Escaping the Pink Ghetto

One Sunday morning, at the preposterously early hour of 8 A.M., I found myself addressing a crowd of six hundred or so women at the Grace Hopper Celebration of Women in Computing conference in San Jose. I was on a panel with several women CEOs of Silicon Valley software companies. Our topic for the morning: "The Future of Computing: Seizing the Future We Want."

I generally like public appearances. Computer industry panels and speeches are a primary means of reaching entrepreneurs. The questions raised tend to be fairly stimulating, and there's something to be learned from fellow panelists. Besides, it's kind of fun to get up and speak to a receptive crowd, which is the usual case at conferences like these. After all, entrepreneurs are looking for guidance and money, and we offer both.

It's usually fun. But it was rather discouraging this time. First, it must be said that I generally try to avoid the whole "woman" issue. It comes up quite a bit because female CEOs and female venture capital partners are, as the saying goes, scarce as hens' teeth in the computer industry. As one of very few female technology venture capitalists in the Valley, I can tell you that being a woman is both an advantage and a liability—an advantage because you are noticed, a disadvantage because sometimes you don't feel completely like part of "the club."

The computer industry and the venture community are some of the better meritocracies around. Entrepreneurs are completely merit-oriented and show no prejudice at all. Basically, they want help, and if you can give it, you could be a Martian with purple spots for all they care.

But meritocracy or not, the computer industry still boasts very few women CEOs, a situation that's out of line with the overall percentage of women in the computer industry. So I agreed to join the panel in San Jose to talk about the issue. My fellow panelists were women CEOs of software companies in the Valley; I was the only venture capitalist. Looking over the panelists' names while I prepared my speech, I recognized only one. The rest headed small software companies that were new to me. The audience was composed primarily of women, many of them graduate students in computing who wished to build careers in the computer industry.

A friend of mine, a writer on the computer industry and a fairly well-known academic, was leading the panel. She gave me complete freedom concerning my topic, so I went straight to the heart of the matter: "Why Aren't There More Female CEOs?" I chose this question not just to engender conference debate, but because it truly puzzled me.

The old argument was that women were not leaders in the computer industry because they did not major in engineering or computer science in college. But in my speeches to undergraduate and graduate students at Stanford and Berkeley, I had noticed that by and large such classes were at least half composed of women. Besides, it's not as though all male CEOs have an engineering or computer science degree; some are just smart and aggressive, Bill Gates being a perfect example.

Another argument is that women don't have enough management experience. This is patently false. Most of the technology companies that I know in the Valley have one or more women as part of their executive team. Many of these women have been executives for years and are more seasoned than many of their male colleagues. There's no reason, on the surface, why they shouldn't be CEOs.

So what's the reason? I launched into my speech, partly to pose the question for the audience to consider, partly in search of the answer for myself.

"Why aren't there more women CEOs?" I asked. It was clear to me that the opportunities were there. Most women, however, didn't step up to the responsibility. Why? Did they lack confidence? Did they fear competing for the job? Were they sole contributors and not team players, and therefore held back? What was it?

None of these reasons was the root cause; on the basis of many discussions with both men and women, I argued that for some reason women didn't seem to like the loneliness of the job. Women managers wanted respect, yes, but even more they wanted to be liked—something men appeared more prepared to give up in order to be respected and have power. I knew this was not a politically correct position, but that was how the situation appeared to me.

Then the other panelists began to speak, throwing out their prepared texts and leaping straight to my question. There were a variety of opinions offered, but I found the reaction of the young women in the audience most surprising. They responded to my question with some questions of their own: "Why do you assume that women want to be CEOs anyway? Why can't women just be academics or vice presidents of human resources or whatever if that's what they want?" After all, they asked, weren't these just as honorable professions as being CEO of a technology company?

I was disappointed to hear this response. Though it seemed to me that women have historically chosen not to pursue positions of power, I had hoped that, given the strides that have been made in the workplace, younger women wouldn't have the same fears and reluctance to lead. Many people have fought for many years to ensure that women have the same opportunities at work that men do. Now a small number of the newest generation of working women were saying they just plain weren't interested in reaching the highest levels of management.

A full year after the conference, I still don't know how to assess what I learned. Maybe my views—that women should push to achieve the highest level of accomplishment they can—are an anomaly. But I would love to see women fight for their advancement in the same way founders fight for their companies—to their last bit of energy. Many women still won't earn top CEO spots or be the best venture capitalists ever. But failure to reach the top should never be for lack of heart.

Chapter 5

Does Your Angel Have Wings?

In the spring of 1998, venture capitalists and entrepreneurs in the Valley began reading stories in their morning newspapers predicting the death of venture capital. Articles on this topic began appearing in papers up and down the journalistic food chain, from the *San Jose Mercury News* to the business bible, the *Wall Street Journal.* The story: Start-up companies in Silicon Valley no longer needed venture capitalists, because local "angel" investors were providing them with all the cash they required.

Who were these "angel" investors? In a word, they were local entrepreneurs who had made millions in the raging bull market of the 1990s and were ready to invest in new start-ups. With their newfound wealth, many had moved on to less pressing duties in their companies or to actual retirement. What better way to invest their time and money than in helping other start-ups get going?

Individual angel investors had been around for a while, sporadically investing their time and capital. But by the mid-1990s, angel investors were wielding increasing influence—partly because there were simply more of them, but also because they began to group together in consortiums and make decisions much like venture partnerships. Some groups were quite large. One, called the "Band of Angels," numbered about seventy-five investors.

The stories about the demise of early-stage venture capital and its replacement by angel investing were controversial, so they made good headlines. But none of the key parties—the angels, the venture capitalists, or the founders—were interested in that kind of outcome. The funding business has become too large, fast-growing, and symbiotic for that.

One story predicting the demise of venture capital was about a local East Bay company, Sendmail, which had just received funding from the Band of Angels. The gist of the article was this: Sendmail was a company that fit the profile of a classic venture capital investment, but its founders had turned to the angels for funding. Did this signal a trend? Were venture capitalists becoming obsolete?

Sendmail had been created in 1979 as a nonprofit corporation aimed at creating great new software to be shared. This type of free software, or "shareware," predated the general public cognizance of the Internet and the World Wide Web. The technologists who created the software were focused on its quality rather than profit; they freely shared it via electronic bulletin boards.

As shareware, Sendmail had become the server of choice for e-mail on the Internet. By the late 1990s it had an impressive 70 percent penetration among server-side e-mail software. It faced competition from Microsoft Exchange and from Lotus Notes, but these were heavy-infrastructure and proprietary-standard products being pushed by large companies to make a profit. Sendmail had been about quality, and its product had been produced for love rather than money—love of great technology, and of the idea of free access to that technology.

When Internet stocks started to set the stock market ablaze, many of those formerly shareware products went commercial. Sendmail was one of these. The company decided to keep the product in the public domain—available for free to universities and the like—but to charge corporations for its use and for upgrades. Realizing that it needed capital to fund future growth, Sendmail began talking to a few investors, traditional venture firms as well as angel investors.

Investors liked the company. Although wary of investing in a company that would compete directly with Microsoft and its Exchange server business, we and others were intrigued with the quality of Sendmail and its penetration in the market.

Then the story appeared in the *Mercury News* and the *Wall Street Journal:* Sendmail had accepted $6 million from angel investors. The press jumped on the story: Venture capitalists replaced by hardworking angel investors! The status quo replaced by the up-and-coming renegades!

It's a sexy story, and it's easy to see why it would appeal to journalists. And indeed, angel investors, as well as family and friends, are a completely legitimate source for funding an early-stage company. Sendmail chose the unusual option of being completely funded by angel investors, even on later rounds.

But founders should make sure they realize that angel funding differs from working with venture capitalists. Professional venture capital carries with it a commitment to subsequent funding if the company is generally meeting its goals, even in worsening market conditions. Angel investing usually involves funding just to get the company started, not to see it through hard times.

Professional venture capital investing also usually involves a serious time commitment on the part of a partner and the partnership to help you, the entrepreneur, build your company. This time commitment relates to being your partner: helping you to recruit a great management team, strategizing with you on the company's future direction, helping you to identify funding sources, introducing you to corporate or marketing partners—whatever is required to help you and the company be successful.

Your venture investor also makes a long-term commitment to your company. This makes sense because the venture capitalist is in the business of helping to start and support companies. Angel investors generally cannot make this same type of long-term partnership commitment involving both time and money. Angels are usually more interested in providing you with capital to get started so that venture capitalists will assist your company—with time and money—in later rounds.

Another key difference is that venture capital brings with it a history, the knowledge gained from starting hundreds of companies, not just one or two. Among our partners, we have seen most of the mistakes that can be made. That knowledge can be used to assist you when faced with similar problems.

There is another mistaken notion surrounding venture capital and angel investing. That myth is that angel investors do early, or seed-stage, rounds because large and successful venture firms no longer wish to do this type of early-stage investing but would rather focus on more well-formed companies and larger, later-stage investments.

This notion is completely wrong. At IVP we partner with entrepreneurs at the earliest stages of forming a company. We often provide what we call incubation space to allow the entrepreneur to have a place close to us to start working on the idea before a team has even been recruited. However, if a company has chosen to get angel funding to get the idea started, that will be no impediment to working with them.

Like most things, choosing angel or venture investing is usually not an either-or decision. The key is to recognize which option, or combination of options, is best for your situation.

People

Chapter 6

People Are to a Business What Location Is to a Restaurant

Like most venture partnerships, the partners at IVP hold an annual off-site strategy session at some remote location—Sedona, Arizona, or Pebble Beach, for example—to spend time together thinking strategically and looking at the proverbial "big picture." One venture firm uses this time to do really interesting and challenging activities together—taking flying trapeze lessons, for example, or formula car racing. We at IVP use this time to discuss the broad issues that may affect our future investments, issues such as the state of venture capital, the world economy, and the future directions of technology.

These retreats are meant to help the partners step back and take a "macro" view by getting out of the office, relaxing, and getting to know one another better. The resorts are beautiful—at the Lodge at Pebble Beach, for example, the windows in the rooms look out over a tranquil bay. But on the other hand, we're there to work, so we spend most of the day sitting in a room talking to one another rather than taking much advantage of the activities the resort has to offer. The idea is to get us thinking "out of the box."

The discussions are wide-ranging, but frequently they center on the primary elements necessary to creating a successful company. At the heart of the debate is a key question: Which is the most important element in a successful company, the market for its product or the people who run it?

There is great debate and a wide spectrum of opinion on this point within the venture capital community. On one end of the spectrum is Don Valentine, a partner at Sequoia Capital. Don is an experienced older guy with a reputation for being pretty tough on his companies. One entrepreneur reports that every time his company sent Don (who sat on the board of directors) its financials, Don would send them back with a big red circle around the number of months for which the company had sufficient cash. Don, who has been a very successful venture capitalist, has often publicly explained that he believes that markets are more important than people in the successful company equation.

He illustrates this theory using the example of Cisco Systems. Don invested early in Cisco, a company that makes Internet networking products and software, after the company was turned down by numerous venture capitalists who were, for one reason or another, unimpressed by the founders. While other venture capitalists were focused on the shortcomings of the team, Don was one of the few who saw the tremendous potential of the router market.

Though he and Cisco's board were later forced to replace the founders, Don apparently called it right: Cisco has since become one of the largest and most successful companies in the technology industry, with annual revenues of more than $8 billion. It has become to communications what Microsoft is to software. In Don's eyes, the market opportunity was what mattered—and all those venture capitalists who turned down Cisco because of issues with the founders were too shortsighted to see that.

Arthur Rock, a partner at Arthur Rock & Co., and an early investor in Apple Computer, appears to lean more toward the opposite end of the spectrum—people rather than markets. While he has publicly stated that a good market opportunity is important, he also believes that a great management team will find a good opportunity, even if they have to make a huge leap from the market that they currently occupy. He too could cite many examples to support his position, one of which is Apple. While it's hard to argue that Apple did not have a great market opportunity, Steve Jobs is certainly among the top tier of entrepreneurs, as evidenced by his multiple successes and his revival of Apple's fortunes after the company went through a difficult period. My husband, David Liddle, who is a successful entrepreneur himself, believes that Steve is one of the best marketing minds in Silicon Valley. I agree.

And the debate goes on. It reminds me of the old baseball maxim: "Good hitting beats good pitching and vice versa." Who's to say, on any given game day, which will lead to victory?

IVP is moving very much toward Don's position—that a large and fast-growing market is critical. But I personally also have a tendency toward backing great people. My hope is that great people will have great ideas that will attract other great people. The example that really solidified this point in my thinking was my very first Internet investment. Because it changes so rapidly, the Internet market, more so than many other markets, really highlights how flexible, competent people can succeed.

In the summer of 1994, when IVP began investing in the Internet, I was thinking about the Web's ability to provide a great medium for interactive entertainment. Playing games on computers was already a hugely popular pastime—but it was clear that it would be much more entertaining if people could play against one another and interact, rather than just playing against the computer. When Brian Apgar, a former vice president of engineering at a computer hardware company, joined IVP that summer as what we call an "entrepreneur-in-residence" (EIR), he helped us look at possible investments and began working on interactive entertainment on the Web. Later, when he came up with an idea for a service to provide multiplayer gaming on the Web, we called the company Mpath (later renamed HearMe).

Very quickly, this new market, like most new Internet market opportunities, took on the incandescent glow of hot opportunity. Five or six companies, some of them venture-backed, sprouted up and started to pursue the market at the same time.

Since HearMe's founders were engineers or developers with little business and management experience, the company hired a professional recruiter to assist in hiring our CEO. We hit the jackpot in Paul Matteucci, a division manager at Adaptec, a local publicly traded PC peripherals company. Paul was an unusual choice: it wasn't exactly standard practice to pluck a senior manager from a more staid and stable industry like peripherals to head a start-up in a wild and woolly, brand-new market like Web entertainment.

Paul is a feisty Italian, a masterful cook who seems never to follow a recipe. A short, sturdy man with thinning hair, Paul has a very charismatic presence and a great blend of Mediterranean passion and powerful intellect. Paul, whose early work experiences included helping out at his father's butcher shop and hauling garbage, had gone on to receive a master's degree from Johns Hopkins and an MBA from Stanford. He was a visible and highly courted executive during his time at Adaptec, and he had previously been considered to run a semiconductor communications company IVP had helped start. But he wanted to exercise his creativity, not just his management skills. He was smart, strategic, and a great manager and leader—and he wanted a forum within which he could exercise these talents.

In coming to HearMe, Paul was joining an eclectic team in a brand-new market with no clearly defined business model. He likes to say now that he didn't realize then what he was getting into: while it is probably acceptable to take a risk on an untested team (one that he had no role in recruiting), or a new market, or a difficult new technology, Paul was faced with taking on all three at once.

HearMe had a promising start. The technology, which enabled voice communications over the Net, as well as multiplayer, real-time games such as *Quake,* was impressive. Our early claim to fame was low-latency: you could get our very fat graphics over the Net quickly, while our competitors' were slower. This was hugely important to gamers, of course. When playing *Quake,* if latency is a problem, you're dead in minutes. So that was one clear-cut advantage. And the company had no trouble in its early financing rounds. So far so good. But the trouble began around the business model and the ethic of the Web.

Internet users were used to getting everything for free, since most Net companies used advertising revenues to support free consumer use of their sites. But HearMe chose another route: charging subscriber fees. For users accustomed to accessing Web content for free, this was an unattractive option. Not surprisingly, the company's initial growth was slow and difficult.

To his credit, Paul quickly realized that subscriber fees weren't working and switched to an advertising-based model. But this too was inherently problematic. Advertisers wanted to buy space on sites with a frenzy of Web traffic: lots of users, lots of movement, lots of "reach," in industry parlance. Internet search sites, like Yahoo! and Excite, are perfectly suited for this: users come to the site for a quick hit of information, and they may visit a search site multiple times for short tasks. HearMe users, on the other hand, were fewer in number and stayed on the site for hours at a time. Reach was not a compelling metric for HearMe, and advertising dollars were small at first. So Paul began educating advertisers about a much newer concept: "brand" building on the Net, and the importance of "stickiness"—meaning the user returns to your site several times a day or week, getting exposure to your brand.

To replace the subscription revenues that were lost in the change of business model, Paul created a second business for HearMe, packaging and selling the company's underlying technology, such as billing services, to other interactive sites. He hired a separate team to pursue this opportunity and he managed both businesses, no mean feat for a start-up CEO. At the same time, he pushed his team onward to build the user base for HearMe services.

Now HearMe was pursing two businesses. The company needed additional funding, and Paul managed to raise it, even though HearMe faced clear problems and had no guarantee of success. I believe that the funding came largely in recognition of Paul himself, and of his team's execution.

By the fall of 1998, HearMe boasted approximately three million subscribers to its online service, and its software had been purchased by industry blockbuster firms, including Sony. Momentum favored HearMe now: the stock market reception to Internet companies had been phenomenal, and sure enough, bankers soon began encouraging the company to do an initial public offering, or IPO. An IPO, the first offering of securities (stock) to the public, is a significant milestone, as it means the option holders—the founders, employees, and others who have put hard work into the company—can finally realize cash for their stock. HearMe was getting ready to go public. But here the vagaries of the market intervened.

Unfortunately for Paul, the company, and the investors, the stock market crashed, a victim of jitters over economic meltdowns in Asia and Russia. The window of opportunity for Internet companies to go public slammed shut. After three years of unremitting hard work, re-jiggering the business model, and fighting to crest a limp market wave, HearMe had been dealt perhaps the harshest blow yet, one that might have pushed a lesser CEO to despair. Yet Paul was undeterred and quickly lined up private financing to tide HearMe over until the IPO window opened again.

Over the years, one by one, HearMe's competitors have closed up shop, victims of bad market timing, lack of adaptability, and inability to take calculated risk. Luckily for us, the IPO window reopened early in the spring of 1999. It also looked as if HearMe's early and big investment in audio chat capabilities was the right call. HearMe was leading in one of the hottest areas on the Web—live interaction called "live communities." In February 1999 HearMe filed to go public, marketed its IPO successfully, and nearly tripled its stock price on the first day of trading, reaching $1 billion in market capitalization.

HearMe is where it is largely because of Paul and the team he has developed. And despite all the problems HearMe faced—or perhaps even *because* of them, as they revealed Paul's true mettle—I fully believe Paul will continue to drive a thriving and market-leading company, making us all a great deal of money in the process.

One could certainly argue that my leanings in the People vs. Market debate are not proven by a single example. But the result of my experience is that I am more likely to vote to fund ventures headed by people like Paul—people who rally to prevail despite whatever difficulties undeveloped and changing markets may present them.

Chapter 7

Less Is More, or
Subtraction by Addition

One of the most unusual meetings that we ever had was with the six student founders of Excite. IVP partner M. J. Elmore and I went to meet them for the first time in a modest house that these Stanford graduates were all sharing in Cupertino, a Silicon Valley suburb. These kids—the oldest was a mature twenty-five years old—had been working on some very interesting search technology for more than a year. They had bootstrapped the effort out of their own pockets and were now reduced to living on beans and rice. They didn't even have the money to buy a hard disk with enough memory to test their product. In fact, that was our first investment—we purchased a hard disk for them.

They lived and worked in the house because they could not afford office space. And this house didn't even have a garage. A start-up so poor you couldn't even call it a garage start-up. Even Steve Jobs had a garage.

M. J. and I joked about having to use the bathroom in this frathouse atmosphere. Remember what men's college bathrooms were like? We were afraid to touch anything. But these guys were smart and energetic and driven. It was clear that though they were far from having all the right answers from which to build a business, they had the most important ingredients: intelligence and determination.

Entrepreneurs often fail to understand what is really required of them. In particular, they fail to grasp the notion that in some cases, less might mean more. The Excite guys were dressed in jeans and T-shirts, met us in their living room with its student furniture, had no money for fancy marketing materials or even a powerful enough computer with which to test their product. They had never been employed in, much less managed, a technology business. All of that came later with the help that we, their partners, could provide. Yet Excite, like the Stanford student–founded Yahoo!, went on to become one of the most successful businesses on the Net.

Technology entrepreneurs can wreck the simplicity of their idea by adding complexity to it. Rather than coming to us with just themselves and their bright idea, they believe that we want to see business types as part of the initial management team. So they hire their future CEO or vice president of marketing. Often we like the technology entrepreneur and the plan, but end up in the awkward position of not being able to back the business types selected by the entrepreneur. So don't focus on the trappings—wearing a tie, having a fancy marketing presentation, or an already hired CEO or business team. Focus instead on your idea and why customers will love it and how you and only you can make it happen.

Chapter 8

Make a Decision

1. Make a decision.
2. When you make a decision, stick with it.
3. When there is evidence that your decision is wrong, change it.
4. Never look back.

Make a Decision

Analysis paralysis is a common problem in large companies with rigid bureaucratic structures. Indecision may slow a large company down, but it is death in a start-up. In a small company a manager should not be fired for making the wrong decision so much as for making no decision at all. At least from the wrong decision the manager and the company can learn which is the more correct path to take. Indecision results in no information at all, and the results can be as disastrous as a wrong decision.

Bill Gates committed many tens of millions of dollars to the Macintosh because he believed in the principle of easy-to-use computers. If he were wrong, that decision could have resulted in a large and visible failure for Microsoft. He could have used that knowledge to chart a different path than the one he eventually chose—the path leading to Windows, his own graphical user interface. As it turned out, the reward matched the risk. He made a big and early bet and he was rewarded for it.

When You Make a Decision, Stick with It

Early versions of Windows were pretty bad, but Microsoft stuck with it. For the longest time, Windows was a joke. It was so bad that no one in the industry believed that Microsoft would ever have a world-class product. Windows looked particularly lame when compared to the Macintosh. But Microsoft never became embarrassed by the products that it shipped. The company line was that Windows was good, and it was always getting better. Bill Gates never gave up on his dream of creating and controlling his own graphical user interface. Because he had made a decision to own the graphical user interface for the personal computer, he knew that he had to establish Microsoft's position in this market early.

Eight years and three versions after the first feeble Windows products were introduced, Microsoft had won the graphical user interface war.

If your company is making radical changes—and most Internet companies change their business model at least once in their lifetime—avoid second-guessing yourself. Give your strategy enough time to work.

When There Is Evidence That the Decision Is Wrong, Change It

Microsoft was wrong about the Internet. For the longest time, the company was in denial about it. Bill Gates had spent a tremendous amount of time and money persuading customers to buy Microsoft Windows. Microsoft had also just launched with much fanfare its own proprietary network, called MSN, with a lot of large and visible content partners, such as Disney. The popularity of Netscape's Internet browser and the seemingly unstoppable growth of the Internet were playing havoc with Gates's best-laid plans. Microsoft derided the Net and mocked early pioneers such as Netscape, the creator of the browser software. Microsoft even made a satiric video called "The Web of Wealth," which poked fun at Wall Street's instant love affair with anything Internet, implying that the Internet companies were little more than a shell game with overhyped stock prices. Like I said, denial.

All that changed sometime in late 1996. Bill Gates got religion. For two years he had been wrong about the Internet, and the revolution was about to pass him and Microsoft by. The only answer was to admit publicly to a wrong decision and to change the strategy of the company. Which he did.

Never Look Back

Microsoft came out with all guns blazing. They acquired several Internet companies to get in the game faster. They launched their own Internet browser to compete with Netscape. With its market domination of the desktop, Microsoft had a great deal of weight to throw around, and they threw it. They also had billions to play with while they waited. It felt like George Orwell's *1984*. "Microsoft is not at war with the Internet. We have never been at war with the Internet. We love the Internet." They never looked back.

The lesson here is to look at decisions as objectively as you can. Question yourself occasionally to make sure you are still dealing with reality. The best CEOs lead by force of personality and persuasion, but they remain healthily paranoid that they have made or will make the wrong decision. It is important when leading not to show indecision, yet to retain an open mind. This balance is sometimes tricky.

Microsoft is a giant, but these four simple rules—make a decision, stick with it, change it if it is wrong, and never look back—are relevant to the founder of a company large or small. I could argue that the long view of chipping away at a difficult problem is even more vital to a start-up with few resources than pursuing a series of tactical maneuvers.

Bill Gates is the quintessential entrepreneur of a big company who has always thought and acted like he is in a small company. To date, these four maxims have served him well.

Chapter 9

The Grass Is Not Always Greener

In the last couple of years, a new attitude has begun to seep in around the edges of Silicon Valley: the tendency for an entrepreneur to cut and run in search of better opportunities rather than stick with a company through some of the hard times.

Until the recent convergence of three factors—an incredibly strong economy, a skyrocketing stock market, and the explosive new Internet industry—typical venture-backed companies took years to mature. Now the velocity of everything has changed dramatically. Fortunes that once took years to build can now be won—or lost—in a matter of months. This change, coupled with the incredible number of start-up companies searching for good talent, has led a few entrepreneurs to be on the lookout for ever greener pastures.

My firm has been lucky in having entrepreneurs who have stuck with their companies through thick and thin—and in most cases this strategy has paid off.

Tom H. joined one of our start-ups as CEO from a large, public semiconductor company. Tom was a very high-profile guy. He was a good leader, an incredible salesman, and a very goal-oriented CEO—and it had taken a hefty compensation package to lure him.

The company Tom joined had a great market opportunity, and it had been launched with a lot of fanfare and press coverage. But despite

Tom's impressive sales acumen, leadership qualities, and recruiting abilities, the company had not been able to gain traction and critical mass in its target market, thanks mostly to distribution difficulties. Sales growth was slower than expected. On the bright side, cash was not a big problem: the company had raised over $20 million in its last financing round.

Like all entrepreneurs, Tom hoped his company would rocket into the Internet stratosphere like Yahoo! or eBay. Instead, he had a small, moderate-growth business—nothing to be embarrassed about, certainly, but not the kind of explosive success story of his dreams. And to make matters worse, all around Tom, in the fertile fields of Silicon Valley, there were hundreds of exciting new firms springing up that he could have joined if he had wished.

Tom received many offers to join other companies both small and large. Instead, he passed up those opportunities to stay and find a long-term buyer/partner for his company, a partner who could provide the necessary distribution channel to make his company's products successful. This outcome, while not the rocket ship that he had envisioned, is viewed as successful for both him and the company.

Before the Internet revolution, executives considered themselves successful if they were simply part of a growing and well-financed company. They expected that it would take a lot of hard work, luck, perseverance—and yes, time—to make a company a success. Luckily, some of this attitude still remains in Silicon Valley.

Gary Steele was a young manager whom we recruited from Sybase to join an Internet start-up called Netiva, later renamed Portera Systems. Shortly after joined as CEO, Gary assessed the company's prospects and determined that its current product did not offer an especially large market opportunity. This would have been discouraging to many managers. But Gary, recognizing that he had good raw material in the development team and marketing resources of the company, decided in effect to restart the entire company in a totally new direction.

This was a hugely daunting task, but although Gary was almost certainly being recruited to join other start-ups and could have chosen to bail, there was something in him that insisted on seeing it through. As he told me, he was in it to build a billion-dollar company or go out of business.

When Gary joined, the company had a high burn rate due to the cost of supporting a national direct sales force. Burn rate in a start-up company is defined as the amount of capital consumed each month in thousands or millions of dollars. The burn rate had to come down, so Gary was faced with one of the harder tasks a CEO must undertake: he was forced to lay off all the sales force and restructure the company. While this was going on, he and the other senior managers were also conducting research needed for entering a totally new market. Morale could easily have plummeted, but Gary kept everyone focused, working hard, and driving forward. It was a stressful time, and Gary told me he dealt with it by running ten miles every day—it was the only way he could stay sane and sleep at night.

It may not always be the smartest decision to stay with a company no matter what. There is an opportunity cost to sticking with something and seeing it through. But there's an opportunity cost to leaving too. And there's no guarantee that your new opportunity will be any better than your current one. It's also very hard to predict when a company will hit the "knee" in its growth curve—an inflection point after which sales shoot dramatically up. Plenty of successful companies—AOL is a perfect example—struggle for years before having what suddenly seems like "overnight" success.

Predicting success is never easy. When my partners and I settle in around the conference room table and discuss our probable successes and failures, we rarely turn out to be correct, particularly early on in a company's development. Too much can happen in a market or a company's lifetime. Many companies we think will be great end up mediocre, and companies we thought of as struggling sometimes turn out to be stars.

That said, leaving early is not a great trait in an entrepreneur. In fact, venture capitalists used to refuse to back entrepreneurs who had a reputation for skipping out on a company early in the game. For both the entrepreneur and the investor, the decision to push forward or to sell the company should be fairly unemotional. Together, we should weigh the risk and reward. And we should both keep in mind that the grass is not always greener.

Chapter 10

Set Your Sights Higher
Than Your Own Sandbox

One of the most important roles that an investor, a board member, or an adviser can play is that of unofficial psychologist. The skills of a psychologist—mainly, the ability to discern and understand people's motivations—are some of the most valuable tools in investing.

Motivation is everything in building a company. A few founders are motivated purely by the goal of creating wealth. This can be an excellent incentive, but if it is the sole reason the founder creates the company, it does not usually produce the best results. In general, founders who are motivated purely by wealth often have a short-term view, leading them to make tactical rather than strategic decisions. Their companies may succeed in producing substantial short-term payback, but they generally do not develop into the kind of large and successful companies that create the greatest value for founders and investors over time.

At the same time, a healthy desire for wealth creation is a necessary goal. Otherwise, the investment is dominated solely by the psychological needs of the founder—needs that can be as diverse as personal achievement, a desire for power, or even a search for purpose in life. The company that becomes the personal sandbox of the founders almost never becomes hugely successful.

My very first investment as a partner at IVP was that kind of sand-box deal. From my days as a software industry analyst, I had a pretty good feel for management teams, but I was truly a babe in the woods when it came to venture capital. I was green, and I made mistakes, the first and worst of which was not recognizing the motivation of the entrepreneurs in whom I was investing.

George W., the CEO, lives an austere life. He had been raised by his parents, both university professors, to live and think frugally, and his management of the company reflected his roots. In the midst of the bull-market-driven excesses of many of his colleagues and competitors, he drove an old Japanese hatchback and considered a week at the beach to be an extravagant vacation. Money just didn't seem important to him.

The first signs of trouble came when we began negotiations to make the investment. Unfortunately, because it was my first deal as a venture capitalist, I was too inexperienced to recognize what those signs might come to mean. Right off the bat, the negotiations on the current and future status of the company's founders were complex. Later, we got stuck in protracted debates about every single point, whether it was major or minor.

Second, the concentration of ownership was almost totally with the founders—again, not an unprecedented state of affairs. But unlike the situation in most high-technology companies, these founders had shared little of the company's equity with the other employees. This is not a method for attracting a great management team.

But the market was growing, the team's technology was good, and they had a history of success in creating products. About five months went by, and out of the blue we received an offer of $50 million to buy the company. At the time, the company had about $2 million in cash, and revenues of around $1 million. The offer—for what's called a pooling of interests, where the acquired company would receive the stock of the acquiring company—came from a public software company that had annual revenues of several hundred million dollars.

I couldn't believe our luck. What a beautiful bluebird had just flown in our company's little window! At this point I believed that the reward being offered far outweighed the risk of our building a large company. George disagreed. He believed that his company would one day outgrow the acquiring company, and he refused the offer.

The following year, the company wishing to acquire us was itself acquired by another public company for over a billion dollars—approximately three times its market capitalization. If we had accepted the earlier acquisition offer, our company, with very little effort, would have been worth $150 million.

Two years later, history would repeat itself. By that time the company's fortunes had not fared so well: our industry was in a slump, many of the company's products had been late to market, and many had not sold very well. Despite an investment from a large strategic partner, the company was on the brink of running out of cash.

Luckily, despite our rather precarious position, another ready and willing public software company was prepared to buy us. They liked our development team and our future projects. With our revenues hovering around $4 million, we received an offer of around $40 million for the company. Again, it would have been a pooling of interests whereby we would receive the acquiring company's public stock. The best aspect of this is that the stock can be sold for cash, or its value may multiply if the acquiring company does well in the future or if the acquiring company is itself acquired.

As board members, we have an obligation to look out for and represent all of the shareholders' interests. I felt that to accept this offer was right for all shareholders—founders, employees, and investors alike. Given the state of the industry, a great price was being offered. The board tried to convince George to accept. But he was still thinking about his "sandbox," not of the benefit to all of his shareholders. Despite the company's bleak future prospects, George flatly refused to sell. He wanted to remain CEO, and he wanted the company to remain independent.

A few months later the company ran out of cash. At that point it had to be sold just to keep jobs for its employees and to cover its liabilities. For several years of hard work and pain, the founders and employees ended up with nothing and the investors lost almost ten million dollars.

This did not have to be the outcome. George and the company had several chances at success. He just lost perspective in his sandbox.

There is a lesson in this story. The key to success for small companies is to adapt—your strategies, your products, and your people, whatever it takes to succeed. It is important not to let your ego as a founder or CEO hinder this adaptive process. If you do, your company will fail to adapt to changing market and competitive conditions and will almost certainly fail to achieve the success that you so richly deserve.

Chapter 11

Take Me to Your Leader

Mark S. had just walked out of my office looking really dejected. Things looked pretty bleak for him right at that moment: he had come to tell me that the cofounder of his Internet start-up wanted to quit. The company was only ten months old and already one of the founders wanted to quit. How had things gotten so bad, particularly when everything had looked so rosy just six months before?

The sequence of events that had led to Mark's company nearly crumbling was innocuous. But it taught me a very important lesson. That lesson is about leadership—about what it takes to nourish and grow a small company into a large one. I just had never seen up close and personal what happens to a company without leadership. It's like watching a headless body that flails around and injures itself in the process.

Mark was a smart, likable guy who had obvious entrepreneurial instincts. As a child he had been something of a bridge prodigy. He was quite bright and he found it somewhat difficult to be patient and to suffer fools gladly. When he came up with an idea for an Internet company to provide customer support primarily for electronic commerce companies, it was obviously a good idea. We helped him recruit technical cofounders who would be responsible for building the company's product.

But who should be CEO? Historically, the evidence would show that most founders need to recruit an experienced CEO. Many companies have failed because the founder refused to recognize this fact. The important concept to remember is this: everyone (founders, investors, managers) should want to make the company succeed; ego should not be a factor in decisions.

It's a rare but desirable situation if the founder has the necessary skills to be CEO. It's desirable because the threat of a personality conflict between a separate CEO and founder is eliminated. Also, the founder usually has a "never-say-die" attitude that often carries the company through later hard times. Though recruited CEOs are often better managers, they sometimes don't have the same level of commitment as the founder of a company.

The reason that founders often don't make good CEOs is that many founders have technical backgrounds, and they don't have the necessary management experience and skills to develop and guide a large team. So while venture capitalists do generally prefer to make a competent founder the CEO, ultimately the only point is that the company be successful, whoever is in charge.

Mark wanted the CEO title for a simple reason: he had never before been a CEO, so he wanted to try it. Mark was a marketing guy, and we investors reasoned that the company would be spending the first few months refining its marketing position and customer profile. So we believed there was little downside risk to Mark's being the founding CEO.

The first few months of the company's existence went pretty well. The team identified potential strategic directions and products and recruited lower-level engineers. The board was briefed often on product progress. Things seemed to be rolling along according to plan.

The trouble began with what is often a CEO's first leadership test—executive recruiting. Silicon Valley is a horrific place to recruit; every good technology executive has ten or more offers from venture-backed technology start-ups. In the technological fertile crescent of the Valley, it is exceedingly difficult to get great executives to shut off other options and commit to your company. So executive recruiting is a first, crucial test of a CEO's ability to build a successful company.

Mark made a fairly classic recruiting mistake: he failed to make a great candidate feel like he or she was the one. One of Mark's characteristics was that he always held many differing options in mind at the same time, a quality that would explain his success in bridge, a game that requires considerable mental juggling. He could do this easily, but he didn't seem able to communicate those options to the rest of the team and choose only one to back when the timing was appropriate. So, in an admittedly tough recruiting environment, he was having some trouble recruiting top talent.

This was a problem, but not necessarily an insurmountable one. But the second warning signal came soon: Mark had trouble picking one marketing strategy and sticking with it. At any given time, board members and executives had differing notions of what business the company was in. Again Mark clung to multiple ideas at the same time, trying not to close off his options—and losing his employees and board in the process. Despite the board's demands for clarification, we seemed to have a new strategy every month.

Another problem was the company's focus on the competition. Their product was aimed at the emerging market of Internet customer support, a market that was new and not yet clearly defined, and one in which it was certainly too soon to discern any leaders, much less winners. Yet under Mark's leadership the company appeared obsessed with the positioning of the competition. It was as if Mark was trying to win a race looking back over his shoulder the whole time. It was very destabilizing to the employees, who look to the CEO to lead. If the CEO is distracted from the end goal, it affects the efforts of everyone in the company.

All these things were damaging to the company and worrisome to the board. Mark understood and knew there were problems. He once told me it was like driving a car toward the edge of a cliff: you can see the drop coming but can't do anything to stop moving toward it. He wanted the company to thrive, and he was prepared to do anything to make that happen. But the decisive alarm bell rang when the newly recruited marketing VP left after only two weeks. His biggest complaint: the company lacked focus, clarity, and leadership. The alarm bell was beginning to sound like a death knell.

Mark and the team rallied. Luckily, their product design had progressed and it fit the company's new marketing focus. The board of directors worked with Mark to recruit a new CEO. Things were looking up: the company had a plan and a product, and soon it would have a management team.

But, as with so many of the risk-laden start-ups we spend our days funding, the short spate of smooth riding was deceptive, and it didn't last for long. Even with things beginning to look up, Mark's technical cofounder, Bruce C., had seen enough. While he liked Mark, the product, and the new plan, the recent events had been too destabilizing, too unnerving. He, like so many good executives, was being heavily recruited, and he personally had little invested in being a founder of a company.

Bruce was fairly risk averse. He probably should have been employed by a medium-sized or large company with more stability, rather than in a start-up with all its volatility. So after having committed to the future of the company by coming on board as a founder, he changed his mind and quit. Things couldn't get much worse, it seemed. But as it turned out, Bruce's departure was the catalyst for a real rallying turnaround. We had hit bottom—what other way was there to go but up? The board and Mark together started a search for a permanent CEO; the technical team, despite all of the distractions, delivered a good product on time; and the investors ponied up another million to give the company time to acquire some customers.

With so many factors contributing to the success or failure of a new company, it's easy to forget that some supersede all others in importance. The single most critical success factor for any new company is focus. Without focus, nothing else matters: the troops scatter in all directions, efforts are wasted, and crucial time is lost.

The CEO has to be the one who provides and maintains that focus; this is the essence of leadership. Unfortunately, Mark was unable to provide that early focus. His ability to maintain multiple options, multiple candidates, and multiple strategies in his mind all at the same time, which would be an advantage in other roles within the company, meant that he failed as the CEO to communicate one goal to his board of directors and to his team. That is the lesson of leadership: transmitting which mountain you want the troops to take and making your orders clearly understood.

Markets

Chapter 12

Find Markets the Size of Texas

An interviewer at *Fortune* magazine once asked my friend and colleague Ann Winblad, a partner at Hummer Winblad Venture Partners, what venture capitalists look for in a young company. "We look for markets the size of Texas," she said. And she was right.

We venture capitalists do this for a number of reasons. A large market is very forgiving. If the market is large enough, even a mediocre team and a mediocre execution can still produce a big win. (Despite my bias toward excellent teams over big market opportunities, the benefits of a large market are still indisputable.) Timing is another critical ingredient in success. Even if your market is huge, you still could be several years too early for it. But if the market opportunity is big enough, the payoff for the wait can be worth it.

The best example of this that I have ever seen is the market opportunity that faced AOL in the early 1990s. In the 1980s I had worked in Alex. Brown's Baltimore headquarters as an analyst. Because AOL was located in nearby northern Virginia, I had kept track of the company's progress—through its days as Quantum Computer Services, when it launched a tiny online service called Q-Link, and into its transformation into AOL in the early 1990s, when personal computers started really penetrating into the home. As the fledgling online market evolved, the company evolved with it, changing its name and its focus until it hit on a mainstream market: providing online access and content to average computer users.

One October, at Alex. Brown's annual technology conference in Baltimore, I first met with Steve Case and his management team. At the time, AOL was looking into going public. I thought it would be a good opportunity for Alex. Brown. Though I had about twelve meetings that day, I squeezed Steve and his team into the schedule. We met in a small, stuffy hotel room of a Hyatt hotel overlooking the Baltimore waterfront.

With AOL now the eight-hundred-pound gorilla of the Internet, it's hard to remember a time when the company was just one of dozens trying to cash in on the nascent online wave. But as the eighties gave way to the nineties, AOL was a small company, located behind a car dealership in a bland suburban commercial strip in northern Virginia, with around 100,000 subscribers to its online service. If there was any hint of the enormous success the company would eventually find, it was hidden behind the inscrutable gaze of AOL's cool, cerebral CEO, Steve Case.

Steve never doubted that AOL would one day dominate the online world. In the very early days when he was a twentysomething upstart at the company, fresh out of a marketing job at Procter and Gamble, Steve could be found at industry conferences, hanging around in the back of the room and telling anyone who would listen that his company was going to be huge one day.

But on the day I met with the AOL team, Steve was anxious. AOL needed a quality lead investment banker to make the IPO a success. Hambrecht and Quist was willing to take the company public, but there was a problem: Steve's older brother, Dan, was a partner there. It looked too much like a cozy deal between brothers, which could harm the company's credibility. In this crucial phase of AOL's development, Steve needed to attract a major investment bank.

At our meeting in the hotel room, Steve argued persuasively that AOL, though serving hobbyist customers now, would go mainstream. Modems would become more available in the near future, he believed, and more and more people would be getting online. For my part, I saw that AOL would make electronic mail easier for the masses. I believed the company had a good chance of success, and I hoped that Alex. Brown would do the IPO.

By that time I had transferred from Baltimore to Alex. Brown's West Coast office. Because the firm divides its coverage into East Coast and West Coast (to save employees the hassle of frequent cross-country flights), I knew I couldn't work on the IPO myself. So I referred the company to a banker in our Baltimore office. He met with them to assess their business.

Almost immediately after their meeting, I got a call from Steve. He told me that Alex. Brown and my colleague had turned down—or "passed on," as we call it—the opportunity to take AOL public. "What?" I exclaimed, surprised at the news. "Let me call him and find out what's going on. I'll get back to you soon."

I called my colleague in Baltimore. He explained to me that he had met with the company and just did not see the business opportunity. The company served computer hobbyists, he argued, and a small number of them at that. AOL was providing games, and how important could games be in the future of technology? "This is not like Microsoft, which owns an operating system," he told me, "or other software companies that are providing mission-critical software to their customers.

"Besides," he summed up, "what is this online thing anyway?"

Now that the Internet and e-mail have revolutionized the way we work, play, and communicate, this sounds fantastic. But to understand the decision, you have to put yourself in the shoes of my colleague then. Personal computers had barely started penetrating the home in real numbers by the early 1990s. Online anything was reserved for computer geeks who went into cyberspace for bug fixes. Most Americans did not know what a modem was used for—and in fact, modems were not yet included in all personal computers. It was, on the surface, understandable that the looming significance of this new medium could be missed.

The only difference between my and my colleague's perspective was that I was immersed at that time in the personal computer industry and knew that PCs were starting to penetrate into more homes. I also was an early and enthusiastic proponent of electronic mail. I started using e-mail in 1987 when Lotus published a program, albeit a clunky, difficult-to-use program, that supported it. Most companies had electronic mail within their corporate walls, but e-mail between corporations was awkward at best. You had to know the phone number for corporate gateways, for example—phone numbers that weren't published anywhere. Still, I was able to communicate by electronic mail with the CEOs of the companies that I followed. It was the easiest and surest way to reach them.

In my pre-e-mail days at Alex. Brown's Baltimore office, I was always the last one to leave at the end of the day. Because I dealt with West Coast companies, I always ended up staying late so I could call the CEOs three time zones away. We had a daily 8 A.M. sales meeting during that time, and I was late to every one, dragging in with bags under my eyes. So it's no wonder I loved e-mail right away: it literally changed my life. I was one of very few analysts using it at that time, and because it was so novel to be getting messages from an analyst, the CEOs always responded to them. At last I was able to go home at a reasonable hour. From my own experience I knew that electronic mail was gold.

Although I completely missed forecasting or understanding the industry dominance that AOL would later achieve, my early belief in the importance of e-mail helped give me a positive perspective on the company. I believed my colleague had made a big mistake.

Usually, when a banker decides to pass on an investment, that's the end of the story: a turndown is a turndown. But I was determined not to let this opportunity go by. I went to the head of the commitment committee, which is the entity that must approve all offerings undertaken by the firm. "This is crazy," I told him. "We should do this deal. AOL represents a big market opportunity. I think that online is going to matter one day."

I had some credibility at the firm due to earlier successes and fruitful decisions. But the head of the commitment committee was reluctant simply to overrule a decision made by another banker. He decided to send a third banker to assess the company. She chose to do the offering.

I like to tell this story, because it is hard to believe that AOL, with its $117 billion market capitalization and its $2.6 billion in revenues, once struggled to have anyone, much less major investment banks, believe in its market opportunity. It took a while—nearly a decade—for AOL's market opportunity to ripen. But the opportunity was so large that it was well worth the wait.

How can you tell if you are the next America Online or the next flameout waiting for a market that will never grow? It's very difficult. I never really predicted AOL's ultimate success. In this case, my e-mail experience gave me some insight into AOL: I knew that e-mail, although not yet widespread, was a winning online application and that the pieces to make AOL's market happen—personal computers in the home, modems, and more e-mail use—were in process.

It's often daunting when you are in the early stages of a giant market to tell whether the market will be large. But one thing you can do—something Steve Case did very well—is to truly understand what the available market is. It wasn't long ago that fewer than 10 percent of Americans were online at all. If AOL subscribers at that time represented about a quarter of that 10 percent, or 2.5 percent of the total, it would be easy to say that AOL had a quarter of the available market.

But Steve Case saw it differently. Instead of gunning for the 7.5 percent who were online with other services, he looked at that 10 percent total who were online and calculated that the available market included the 90 percent of Americans who weren't yet online. That was the market opportunity he saw, and that's one of the reasons AOL has achieved its astounding success. Because that 90 percent of a market he envisioned is huge—a market the size of Texas, by anyone's reckoning.

Chapter 13

Are You Selling Vitamins or Aspirin?

As I sat in a board meeting for one of my companies, I found it a little depressing. For the third straight month, sales of the company's Internet customer management product had failed to take off. Luckily, there were some encouraging signs of life. One giant banking customer had signed up for the product, and other large financial service customers had expressed great interest. But inertia in new markets is usually very high, and customer reaction is often slow.

The problem this company's board faced was all too common among venture-backed firms: The risk companies are able to take is simultaneously a blessing and a bane. Venture capital is great in that it allows a company to place early bets on emerging markets, without having to focus on profits at first. The problem is that once a company has taken these risks—and burned through the cash needed to fund them—the market still might not pan out. And when a market is taking too long to emerge, is too competitive, or is too small, often millions of dollars have been invested before that is apparent.

This ability to take risks leads some companies to take chances on their products. Specifically, some companies create products that either aren't compelling or fail to solve a real customer problem. An old venture capital adage calls this "selling vitamins instead of aspirin"—in other words, selling a product that's optional for a customer (and therefore less compelling), rather than one that's a must-have. This lesson really applies to companies selling products or services to other businesses. Consumer products or services, particularly Internet companies, have a completely different dynamic that has to do with convincing a customer through effective marketing and brand building that your company's product or service is a "must-have" rather than a "nice-to-have."

The "vitamins vs. aspirin" problem manifests itself in several ways. One way is when companies build a technology without having identified any need for it. I know this sounds fantastic to anyone who has studied markets—it violates basic rules of marketing logic—but in Silicon Valley it happens all the time. Many products are built because they *can* be built, not because anyone knows that they need them. I'm guilty of building some of these types of companies myself. Then you end up with a product that might seem great on the surface, but for which there's no clear idea what exactly it's for, or what—if any—need it will fulfill.

To combat this tendency, I subscribe to something called the "elevator speech test." It appears trite, but it actually works. The test is this: Can I explain the company's business to someone who's never heard of it—and who's not a technologist—in the time it takes an elevator to travel between floors? If I can't do this, then the business is not usually simple or compelling enough.

Another manifestation of "vitamins vs. aspirin" is the tendency of companies to develop a "point," or partial, solution to a customer problem, as opposed to a "total" solution. In these cases, a company may have a product that satisfies a customer's need—but only part of it. The company will need to expand its focus to address the larger problem, or else it will have to depend on other companies—through partnerships or even by being bought—to become a necessary "aspirin" product.

Now, back to the board meeting. Three years earlier the company had started business in the Internet "push" market, a market aimed at customers who wanted information electronically delivered (or "pushed") to them, rather than having to seek it out on the Web. Initially this market looked like the Next Big Thing, with several dozen push companies, particularly Pointcast, at one time getting a lot of press.

Our company got a few customers and zeroed in on the financial services market, where our product allowed banks to communicate with customers over the Internet—providing, for example, real-time alerts about wire transfers. But then our company contracted one of the syndromes mentioned above. Our technology was great, but it was only a partial solution to the customer's problems. We needed to solve a bank's entire customer management problem, not just the Internet part of it, to achieve real success. We knew we couldn't build the total solution in a reasonable time, so we set about finding acceptable technology companies to partner with.

Assuming we could accomplish that, we would still face a final hurdle. Internet customer management was an emerging market. It was, in a sense, a "vitamin" market that was slowly morphing into an "aspirin" market. This may sound strange, but it's actually much more common than you might think.

In the history of technology, it has happened repeatedly: things that at first seemed optional, or even frivolous, to consumers have become must-haves for the general populace. Telephones, televisions, answering machines, microwave ovens, fax machines, e-mail—all these things were once considered optional items, things that were nice to have, if you felt like spending the money for them. But all of them gradually became must-have items: they changed from vitamins into aspirin.

Sometimes the shift occurred even before people realized it. When AOL suffered a nineteen-hour blackout in August 1996, most assumed the news would be of interest mainly to hardcore Internet users and those who followed the industry. But the massive outcry from irritated users and the tidal wave of press coverage that followed—the AOL blackout led CNN, displacing a story about NASA's finding evidence of possible life on Mars—showed that AOL had become a must-have for its users.

We hoped the emerging market for Internet customer management would go the same way. But would the market ripen before our company died on the vine? We had a little over $4 million in cash, were burning $500,000 a month, and sales were poking along anemically at around $2 million for the year. The company was three years old and had raised a total of $17 million.

This was a key board meeting. It was time for the management and the board together to make a decision. Should we go out and raise more money? Or should we admit that we belonged as part of a larger company's total solution and sell the company?

There were six directors in the board meeting: two founders, the CEO, and three venture capitalists. "What's the projected sales ramp for next quarter?" asked one of the venture capitalists. "Is it higher than this quarter?" It was, the CEO responded, at the same time noting that, as the present quarter itself was in question, how could they be certain about the next? "Is there sales momentum?" I asked. "Yes," answered the CEO—but it was not yet reflected in real orders.

Hope springs eternal in the hearts and minds of both entrepreneurs and venture capitalists. We can see opportunity where no one else can, and we hate to give up on a company. But the problem here was the revenue ramp: it just was not happening fast enough. There were reasons for this. We had recently hired a new vice president of sales and he was upgrading the entire sales team, so we had precious few resources in the field. Both of these factors could easily explain our anemic sales ramp.

The market felt real and compelling—at least for now. The technical team had done a great job building the product. And I believed we would later find other markets where companies needed to communicate with their customers over the Internet. This was just one of those wrenching decisions that you could second-guess forever.

The founders in particular believed that the company needed more resources to realize the product's ultimate potential. They believed that we should sell the company and argued persuasively to do just that. Since the timing was uncertain on this or the other markets, I knew the prospect of real success was a long shot. The team and the investors together decided to interview investment bankers immediately, keeping our fingers crossed that, once we were under the aegis of a larger company, we could hold out until the vitamin market became an aspirin market.

Chapter 14

You Must Think Big
to Be Big

Ken Hawk was all you could want in an entrepreneur. He had all-American good looks: he was tall, clean-shaven, and physically fit from years of playing hockey (which he, in true time-pressed entrepreneur fashion, chose because it's the "most effective" form of exercise he knew, providing the biggest results in the least amount of time). He had an unrelentingly positive outlook, coupled with a kind of boosterish enthusiasm for Reno that contrasted with the more fashionably jaded style of Silicon Valley. He was smart, hardworking, had high integrity—and in four years he had successfully built his mail-order and catalog business (which became iGo) to $16 million on very little invested capital.

Ken, who had graduated from Stanford Business School a few years back, had built his company as an outgrowth of a study he'd done for one of his classes. He was proud of his growing company, and, considering its success, he had earned the right to be. So it was a bit of a shock to Ken that when he came to us for an investment, he at first received somewhat of a neutral reaction from the partners.

The key issue we had with Ken was how he viewed his potential market opportunity. His current market—selling batteries for laptop computers and cell phones by telephone, through the mail, and on the

Internet—was fine. We just believed that Ken needed to think bigger. Venture capitalists are in the habit of taking calculated risks. We know that it is just as difficult to build a small company as a large one, so we would rather take the risk on building a large company in a large market, even if that market does not yet exist.

Ken was at the heart of a market opportunity that we were very interested in pursuing: electronic commerce. Electronic commerce—essentially online marketing and selling—looked to be the next huge opportunity arising out of the Internet, poised to displace brick-and-mortar businesses. The best and most visible example of this market displacement was Amazon, the Seattle-based stock phenomenon that sold books, CDs, pet food, drugstore items, and other merchandise online.

Ken had to learn to think about his target customer in a bigger way. Instead of looking at his customers as simply purchasers of replacement batteries—a narrowly defined need—he had to see them as mobile users with a broad set of needs. And he needed to focus most of his future efforts on driving sales through his Web site. At the time, Web site sales accounted for only a small percentage of his overall sales. We believed that if he didn't grab the high ground—selling a variety of products and services to a broad base of mobile users over the Internet—some other company was going to plant its flag ahead of him.

Because Ken had taken very little investment capital to date, just a few million dollars from a New York investor, he had tried to run his business with a target of near-term profitability. This is generally a good idea, but not in exploding new markets like electronic commerce. On the Web and in these new emerging markets, market share—*not* profitability—is often the key to success. Explosive revenue growth is the name of the game, however you have to achieve it.

Amazon itself was a poster child for this concept. While its revenue growth was enormous, the company had lost tens of millions of dollars and had no date for projected profitability. Yet Amazon's valuation was tremendous, thanks to the potential electronic commerce platform it represented for all kinds of businesses.

Ken needed to look at his business more like Amazon founder and CEO Jeff Bezos did. Rechargeable replacement batteries for laptops and cell phones is a commodity business—meaning it's hard to differentiate your product from others'—but then again, so is books. Amazon had managed to differentiate itself through breadth of book selection, customer service, and technology that helped propose new books to customers. Ken could differentiate in a similar manner. To be really big, Ken had to think more like a destination Web site for mobile users, rather than simply as a seller of batteries. This meant he had to be ready to cross-sell other complementary products when a user came to his Web site.

This was something Bezos understood well. He saw Amazon's value as a congregation point for customers ready to purchase all sorts of good over the Web. Getting the customers there was the hard part, and Amazon had solved that problem in spades: later, the company could simply capitalize on the customer presence. For his part, Ken needed to be much more aggressive than he previously had been to become a major player on the Web.

None of this message was surprising to Ken. Like I said, he was smart, ambitious, and driven. But this company had been his baby. And the baby needed a push to start walking. We named one of our partners who is an experienced and successful entrepreneur to help Ken begin to think bigger about his market opportunity. We helped Ken to rename his company iGo, broaden his message, focus on electronic commerce, and ultimately position it to go public.

Ken's company is a good example for any entrepreneur. When you are attempting to enter a new or emerging market, such as electronic commerce, it is helpful to use analogies of other corporate success stories. These analogies let you both (a) size up a potential market and (b) highlight the kinds of difficulties you may encounter. If several companies have tried to enter a market and none has been successful, this should tell you something about the level of risk inherent in that market. If several companies are competing in a market and none has risen to leadership or grown very large, this may tell you that it is nearly impossible for a company to get large in that market. In that case, choosing a new market opportunity would be wise.

This same rule can be used on business models. Ask yourself this: What successful company has created a large and growing company using your proposed business model? If the answer is none, the odds are against your being the first one to do so. This doesn't mean it can't be done, but it does mean the level of risk is very high. So if you do choose to take a chance on an untested business model, the rewards at the end should be consummate with the enormous risk you're taking.

For a lower-risk proposition, it's best to examine and learn from other, successful business models. The examples don't need to be ones only within your target market. But analogies can help you to reality-check your assumptions about your company's potential market size, market characteristics, and business model.

In Ken's case, the Amazon analogy sent him a powerful message: it showed him that he was aiming too low. To be really successful, he had to aim his sights higher, by thinking about owning a customer demographic, the mobile user. He also needed to think about building a platform for a variety of future products and services to obtain explosive revenue growth, not just moving his retail battery business to the Web. Ken immediately began to take steps to put into practice a lesson that he already knew—he began to think big, so that he would one day be big.

Chapter 15

It's Turtles
All the Way Down

I am wondering as I begin writing this chapter whether the Internet stock market bubble will outlast the publication date of this book. Internet stock valuations are a hot topic of discussion. Why? Because companies such as Amazon or Priceline, which have yet to—and may never—turn a profit, are worth billions of dollars.

This remarkable flow of money into relatively unproven new companies is the subject of editorials, hundreds of Internet message boards and newsgroups—even a satirical poke in the *Doonesbury* comic strip, where character Mike Doonesbury tries to explain the Internet bubble phenomenon to his young daughter. "In the Internet business, profitability is for wimps," he tells her. "It means your business plan wasn't aggressive enough. It's okay to lose a lot of money, as long as it's on purpose."

The Internet explosion and subsequent stock-price bubble has caused a major rift in Silicon Valley. More specifically, it's a rift among the venture capitalists themselves, a division between the haves and the have-nots. The haves are those venture capital firms that made early Internet investments; the have-nots did not.

First, it must be said that the term "have-not" is a bit misleading here, mainly because it characterizes venture capitalists who are essentially successful, but just not in on the explosive, unprecedented paybacks made possible in the new world of high-flying Internet stocks, where one successful Internet company investment can result in a return more than a hundred times as great as any other of your start-up company investments.

Entrepreneurs share in this have-not feeling and feel like failures if their company doesn't go public within one to two years of creation and gain an enormous market valuation. Founders feel like failures if their company doesn't have the success of a Yahoo!, which was started in 1994, went public two years later, and now is worth $37 billion.

The phenomenon where young workers—from the receptionist on up—become instant millionaires after a year or two of work has started legions of employees salivating, dreaming of a big, quick payoff. If the old American work ethic was "Work hard and long to climb the ladder of success," the new paradigm is "Go fast for the big win."

After all, how's an entrepreneur supposed to feel when a company like Hotmail—a provider of free e-mail, *without revenues or probably even a plan for revenues*—is purchased by Microsoft for more than $400 million? What does it do to the motivation of an entrepreneur who has carefully built his company—gone after a good market, created a great product or service, and in three years built a company with revenues of, let's say, $10 million—to be worth maybe $100 million at most? No matter how impressive their achievement may be, such entrepreneurs can't help but feel like failures next to the Net wizards.

The World Wide Web has jokingly been called a creation that gives a new meaning to the term "black hole"—as in, a black hole into which companies pour untold sums of money, chasing the promise of future profits. Many Web sites and Web-related companies—Amazon, newspaper-affiliated sites like washingtonpost.com, and even billion-dollar companies like AOL—have struggled to achieve profitability.

Although this has changed somewhat lately, one of the obstacles in the past to profitability has been the reluctance of mainstream advertisers—Coca-Cola, Procter and Gamble, Nike, and others—to purchase huge numbers of ads on Web sites. They simply did not yet have enough faith in the medium to take a major leap and shift major advertising dollars from mass media to the Web. This is changing, but television advertising and other types of advertising still dwarf the Web. So what you have instead is primarily Web-savvy companies advertising on Web companies.

Web sites measure their success in terms of "eyeballs," industry slang for the number of users looking at a site. Never mind that having more people look at a Web site doesn't necessarily translate into more money coming into the site.

I am reminded of an old story:

An old woman is asked, "What holds the earth up?" She responds gravely: "The earth is riding on the back of a giant turtle."

The questioner takes this in, then asks, "Well, what holds up the giant turtle?" To this, too, the woman has an answer: "It's standing on the back of another giant turtle."

"Yes," the questioner persists, "but what is that turtle standing on?"

"It's no use trying to trick me, sir!" crows the old woman. "It's turtles all the way down!"

Perhaps the present-day variation, then, is: "It's eyeballs all the way down!"

The Net is having a profound effect on the way we live and work. And along the way, it appears to be rewriting the time-honored rules of investing in and building a business. Is this a permanent shift? Or will the bubble burst? It's still too early to tell.

What is clear is that the stock market is giving Internet companies access to large amounts of capital very easily. These companies can then invest in their future growth at the expense of current profits. Most of the most successful and largest Internet companies could be profitable if they chose. But at this point, the stock market is rewarding revenue growth and market share.

It appears that enough people are believing in the "eyeballs all the way down" theory to help keep this remarkable bubble intact for some time to come.

Chapter 16

The Next Big Thing

The Internet and software industries, like most others, are subject to fads. I have seen a couple of huge investment fads sweep these industries within the last ten years. Remember pen computing? How about Internet "push" companies? And now, as I write this, there's a craze for hosted-application or outsourced software companies where software is rented as a service by the month rather than purchased as a product.

I like to think of these fads as "fashion" investments. Fashion investments have their own kind of investment logic. The focus is more on the industry or the type of investment—such as the team, or the timing of the market, or the price—rather than on the basic characteristics of the investment. They tend to last about twelve to eighteen months, after which the bloom is usually off the rose and investors move on to the *next* Next Big Thing. Just because fads are fleeting doesn't mean they're not worthy investments. It just means that, for a time, investors are swept up in collective excitement over a new or novel type of investment.

As a result, investors end up funding a ton of companies in a certain industry or market segment around the same time. This is the case with all of the "fashion" segments listed above. This flood of funding is usually positive in the short term for entrepreneurs (as your company is more likely to get funded) but negative in the long term, as you will face a host of well-funded competition right from the start. The partners at

IVP struggle against this herd mentality, although we too have mistakenly made investments in "fad" industries in the past.

The partners at IVP prefer to invest in what we identify as "waves"—swells made by customer demand. We invest when a wave is first forming and like our investment in the company to peak when a wave is cresting. This usually means anticipating a new market when it is forming. This also means that you usually have to try to lead rather than follow the pack.

One of the most interesting "fashion" industries to be funded within the last ten years was pen computing, a new system that allowed users to write with a penlike tool on a small computer. It was a very cool idea, and it seemed like something consumers would surely love. You could jot down notes into your computer instead of typing them. You could carry your computer with you in your pocket, something unheard of in those days of heavy portables and laptops. You could page through your calendar or look up an address on the fly. What a great idea! It seemed like a sure thing.

Except that it wasn't. Jerry Kaplan, founder of one of the earliest pen computing companies, Go Corporation, liked to say that in the beginning of the pen computing industry, the only money being made was from the pen computing conferences held for entrepreneurs and investors. He was right. Those made money. But the rest of the industry, including the venture capitalists, did not.

Why did pen computing flop? Because the venture capital industry abandoned two of its most cherished principles when it chose to invest in this fad. The first is that the products have to be technically feasible. The second is that there must be some proof that a customer is likely to pay for a technology or a product, assuming it is cost-effectively produced.

From the very beginning of the pen computing craze, the technology was just not there to support the form factors required for a very small and light portable computer. Screen technology was still primitive and heavy. Batteries were still bulky. Processors still generated too much heat. Prices were still way too high. Only a technologist, an early adopter at that, could have loved the first pen computers that were produced. And no one loved the prices.

So what did investors do? Because it was fashionable and because it seemed cool, we rushed in droves to invest almost $100 million in this nonviable technology.

Then the venture capitalists violated a third code: the law of listening to customer feedback. Because this was a brand-new industry—and a brand-new concept—there was no appreciable customer feedback. But later, when the feedback rolled in and it became apparent that customers were not excited with what could be produced at that time at that price, venture capitalists just kept on investing. We were swept up in the fad. Not surprisingly, we all lost our shirts.

What mass hysteria could have possessed the investors and entrepreneurs? There is only one cause for this type of behavior: no one wants to miss out on the Next Big Thing. Rather than risk getting left behind, everyone plunges in together, like lemmings.

Some things *do* turn out to be the Next Big Thing though, the Internet being a prime example. But the Internet, unlike pen computing, violated neither investment rule: first, it was technically feasible and in fact had been in operation for many years, and second, customers loved it.

Unlike pen computing, the Internet represented only an incremental improvement in technology—but one that had a profound social impact. Technologists were not pushing the edge of the envelope with the Internet as they had in pen computing. AOL, Prodigy, and CompuServe had been successfully providing online services for years. Harnessing the Internet was simply taking a step further—like making a large and open AOL. And the price was the best of all—it was free. What was not to like?

Sure, it was a little difficult and awkward to surf. But that improved as the browsers and site management improved. Besides, there were hundreds of thousands of companies hastening that improvement. And as long as it was free, customers felt that they had no right to complain about performance.

If you were an entrepreneur at the beginning of the pen computing industry, it's likely you would have worked very hard for many years and ended up losing everything. By contrast, if you were an entrepreneur at the beginning of the Internet industry, you would likely have sold your company to another Internet company for a large sum—or gone public and suddenly been worth millions of dollars.

Here's a perfect example: In addition to Go Corporation, Jerry Kaplan also founded an early Internet auction company called OnSale. Both companies had the same founder and investors. Both companies were formed in an attempt to cash in on the Next Big Thing. OnSale was a big success, Go a dismal failure. What was the difference? With OnSale, the Internet investment, the investors did not violate their basic principles on technology and customers. And that investment paid off.

So the lesson is not only to observe where the investors and entrepreneurs are flocking, but also to analyze an industry's feasibility in terms of both technology and customer acceptance, before jumping in with both feet.

Business Models

Chapter 17

There Are No More Dolbys

The business model may be the single most important element of a new business. It's the blueprint for the company, and it includes such considerations as:

- How the company will make money
- Who the target customer is, and how much money that customer has to spend on goods or services
- The fragmentation or concentration of competitors in the industry
- Whether any company has been previously successful doing what the new company plans to do—and if not, why not
- The pricing dynamics of the industry
- The distribution channel and its economics
- Dependencies of the company, such as other goods needed to make the product useful or necessary

Getting any one of these wrong can spell doom for a company. Remember: if the business model is correct, often other mistakes can be fixed. But if it's wrong, there's usually no way to prevent ultimate failure.

There's one particular business model that entrepreneurs seem eager to latch on to—and it's one, ironically, that venture capitalists rarely support. I'm talking about licensing. Licensing is a business model in which your company does not "own" the end customer.

There are a few companies that have been successful with a licensing model in the past, including such notable ones as Adobe, Rambus, and Microsoft. But these companies are the exception rather than the rule, and at least two of them required creating an industry standard to achieve success with this model. (Also, the companies spent millions of dollars on ad campaigns to establish the brand. New companies don't have that kind of clout and money.)

Here's how licensing works: Your company owns a technology. You license your technology for a fee to another company, which uses it in a product. That company then has the responsibility of distributing and marketing the product. Sounds good so far, right? Your technology is being distributed in a product, you've been paid for it, and you don't even have to assume any of the distribution and marketing costs. How's that for a low-risk proposition?

But remember: rewards are consummate with risk. There are two major problems with the licensing model. First, you're putting yourself in a dangerous place when the customer's whole relationship to your technology is through someone else's product—in many cases, the customers don't even know your technology is there. If someone else comes along with a similar technology, there's no customer loyalty to help you hang on to your place; you could easily be dumped by the intermediary company, with no real disadvantage to them.

But still, you argue—and believe me, hundreds of entrepreneurs have argued this for generations—just look at the profitability! Because your company doesn't have to pay distribution and marketing costs, the operating margin (meaning the profit after subtracting marketing and sales costs) is terrific.

This is true. But here's the second problem: That profitability comes on revenue numbers that are usually minuscule, because the intermediary company usually pays the licensing company very little for the technology. So the overall profit for the licensing company is quite small. After all, a high margin on a tiny amount is still a tiny amount.

We venture capitalists call this a "lifestyle company": it generates enough money so that the entrepreneur can comfortably maintain his or her lifestyle, but it's unlikely ever to go public. And it's definitely not large enough or protected enough (because the end customer has no loyalty to it) to be backed by venture capital.

All this has been proven time and again. But still entrepreneurs propose this business model for their companies. And when we present the arguments against it, we already know what we will hear in return: the licensing-model devotees' plaintive cry, "But what about Dolby?"

For those of you who don't know the story, Dolby is an example of a moderately successful licensing company. Founded in 1965 by an entrepreneur named Ray Dolby, the company is privately held. Or perhaps it's more accurately described as extremely privately held: more than thirty years after founding the company, Ray Dolby owns 100 percent of the shares, and he reportedly has no plans to offer stock options to employees or go public.

Dolby created a technology that became an audio standard—a technology that was then sold to the consumer by intermediary companies as a kind of audio Good Housekeeping seal of approval. Dolby sound is everywhere. Movie theaters use it, audiocassettes are encoded with it. Its brand is established; its name is recognized by consumers.

So the company has achieved a degree of success. But consider this: in 1997, Dolby had revenues of $100 million. Taking thirty-two years in business to reach $100 million in revenues is far from what we would consider a Silicon Valley success story. Yet Dolby is the example that all entrepreneurs list when trying to prove that licensing is a winning business model.

From venture capitalist's viewpoint, the licensing business model spells death—or, at the very least, insignificance in the target market. If you waste your time or effort creating such a business, you may be able to create your own "lifestyle" or "sandbox" company, but it's unlikely you'll get venture backing or build a really large company.

Chapter 18

Selling a Dollar for Ninety-five Cents Is Not a Winning Business Model

There is one caveat to this chapter title: It's true except in the case of Internet companies, where these days you can apparently sell a dollar for five cents and still win really big. The stock market will accept unprofitable Internet companies if these companies also achieve huge revenue growth and market share gains. In the bull market of the late 1990s, where the stock prices of most technology companies—particularly Internet companies—are in the stratosphere, and companies with no profits in sight are worth millions of dollars, the topic of managing a company's business model and earnings has become a difficult one.

The primary reason Internet-related stocks have become so valuable is investors' belief that these companies represent a new paradigm—a new way of doing business, which will replace the old, outmoded media models such as television and mass-market advertising. Because of this belief, value for these companies is determined by revenue momentum, not earnings. Specifically, it's determined by how quickly investors believe the companies and industries can grow and replace the old, tired media giants. But if your company is not lucky enough to be part of the Internet land rush (and maybe even if it is), a business model that holds water and can sustain your company in future years is crucial.

Dozens of companies and would-be entrepreneurs pass before us each week. One of the key issues that entrepreneurs face is defining their business model. Sometimes venture capitalists do fund companies without long-term sustainable business models, even though we know that a problem with your business model can bring a company down in the long run. However, no cash infusions from venture capitalists or other investors can keep a leaky boat afloat forever.

One of the most common business model problems of non-Internet companies is what I call "selling a dollar for ninety-five cents." This is a situation where the pieces never quite fit together from the beginning to build a profitable and sustainable company. We, along with other venture investors, have mistakenly funded such companies, many of which ultimately go out of business.

Phil D., the CEO of one of our portfolio companies, stood before the partnership for perhaps his final appeal. He had appeared before the partnership asking for money several times in the last few years, as his company required constant cash infusions to keep going.

The reasons for this were pretty clear upon examination of the company's income statement. The company focused on both hardware and some software, and its gross margins (the amount left after manufacturing the product) were skimming along at about 32 percent at best—not a great starting point for profitability. Since a direct sales force was required to sell the product, and spending on research and development was necessary to retain any competitive advantage, operating expenses (the cost to market and sell the product, plus development of new product) were approximately 50 percent of revenues. With this kind of cost structure, the company could not help but lose money at an alarming rate.

Let me make the problem clearer: Say Phil's company earns $1 of revenue. It costs the company $.68 to manufacture its product, leaving $.32 in gross profit. Then it costs the company an additional $.50 to market and sell its product plus some spending on future products. At the end of the day, for each dollar of revenue earned, Phil's company was spending $1.50. This was obviously not a long-term sustainable situation.

At the beginning, Phil's company had an exciting business proposition. Recognizing that Microsoft's newer high-end operating system would become very popular, the company planned to build hardware optimized for that operating system and based on a new, nonstandard chip architecture. The new chips were better in several ways: they were more powerful, faster, and enabled better graphics than standard chips.

As anyone who followed the computer industry knows, the better product is not always the one that thrives. Though the newer nonstandard chip was superior, software developers nonetheless gave increasing support to the more standard chip architecture, eventually making it less and less practical to use the nonstandard chip, no matter how much better it might be. Finally, Phil's company was forced to give in and began using the standard chip architecture. Suddenly the company's chip advantage was gone.

This was a problem. Now Phil's company had to compete with much larger and better-funded hardware manufacturers—and all of them were using the standard chip architecture and the Microsoft high-end operating system. Competitive advantage now began to be about price and manufacturing efficiencies, a game the big guys are always going to win against a smaller, less well-funded competitor.

A lot of money, ours and others', had gone into this company. Despite the setback, Phil was—as entrepreneurs need to be—optimistic. He stood before us again to ask for another infusion to keep his company in business.

It was a difficult meeting. The inclination of our partners is to be very supportive of portfolio companies. But this company had been troubled for some time, and the partners were worried. We were also running into the problem of sunk cost: we had so much invested that it was hard to just give up. But to stay in we would have to give more. This is what makes venture capital so hard. Just at the time you're the most worried about how a company is operating, you have to invest more money—or let the company wither.

Phil answered all our questions thoughtfully, but we could tell he was worried too. I felt sorry for him at that moment. He needed this money desperately, but each time he had gotten money in the past, he had promised it would be the last time. Phil was an intelligent man, and he could see that his business model was not really sustainable for the long term. His costs were too high, and he knew it. His only hope was to ride the popularity of Microsoft's new operating system to much higher unit volumes and therefore revenue levels.

Phil's hope had been that volume levels would increase enough that he could quickly take the company public on the strength of the new operating system's momentum—that way he could garner the cash necessary to keep the company growing. It was a race for the finish line.

But there was one big problem: Phil's company had relatively high fixed costs in its direct sales force and R&D effort. The company needed to spend in these areas to remain competitive and to hit sales targets. It was unlikely that the company could reach the volume levels necessary to really lower its manufacturing costs.

Phil knew this. We knew this. And yet his potential market looked huge. We all wanted a happy ending to this tale. So we backed Phil one more time. Ultimately, we were not successful. Within a year of that meeting, the company had gone out of business.

What can budding entrepreneurs learn from Phil's situation? First of all, unless you are starting an Internet company, don't be blinded into thinking all you need is a huge market opportunity. Your business model still needs to work. Your company will need to have a cost structure that works when you are small.

Venture capital allows companies such as Phil's to take early risks. This risk does not usually apply to business models (except for Internet companies), but rather to technology or to an undeveloped market. It is still necessary to demonstrate that costs will go down as volume goes up, or that the costs are relatively fixed, so that ultimately profitability can be achieved. But sometimes markets look so attractive or a new technology is so innovative that we venture capitalists forget this point. The thing to remember: usually none of us will get rich "selling a dollar for ninety-five cents."

Chapter 19

Keep an Open Mind

Business models are often about creativity. The ones that break new ground—ones that have never been thought of before—are often the most successful. As I mentioned earlier, the level of risk in employing an unproven business model is very high, so the rewards at the end should be worth that risk. Many creative new business models fail. But some succeed and end up being adapted by others in the market.

One good example of this is advertising-based business models for Web companies. In the beginning of the Web, no one had a clue as to how sites could make any money (unless they were charging people to view pornography). At some point, as the popularity of the Web grew, entrepreneurs realized that millions of eyeballs were focusing on their Web sites each day. One of them got the brilliant idea of charging companies to present ads to those captive eyeballs, and voilá—a new industry with a brand-new business model was born.

It wasn't totally new, of course. After all, traditional media companies like newspapers, television, and radio have used advertising as a revenue source for many years. But the application of this business model to the Web was a new spin on an idea. The recognition that services could be given away free on the Web and then supported by advertising was new. And it turned out to be a winner. The Web advertising business is only a few billion dollars. Although that's small potatoes compared to, say, television advertising, Web advertising has been *doubling* in growth every year. And who knows where it will end up? It's possible that Web advertising could one day dwarf other media advertising.

One of the most creative business models I ever saw belonged to an early Internet pioneer named John McAfee. I met John in 1992, in the very early days of the commercial Internet, when I was still with Alex. Brown. His company, McAfee Associates, was providing software that protected computers and networks from viruses. These viruses, which could erase a hard drive or otherwise disable computer functions, were hot news in the early days of the Internet, mainly because the increase in computer networking had made it easier for them to spread.

John was an Internet pioneer, an acknowledged guru of computer viruses and security who wrote several books before he created his software. John had a passion for what he did, and an undeniable energy; his eyes fairly glowed when he spoke about the Internet. I would see this later in a lot of Internet entrepreneurs, but John was the first. And in the beginning he did everything for free, for the sake of the networked world and his love of computing.

John had been a system operator, or sysop, which meant that he ran one of a network of electronic "bulletin boards," where people could get online and post information on a whole variety of interests—from science fiction movies to used cars to antique collecting. Before the Internet became popular, this was the way users interacted. It was a very loosely organized system, not like the streamlined, slicker online offerings of today.

Sysops, who ran the hardware and software needed to keep the bulletin boards going, usually worked at night, on computers in their bedrooms or living rooms. They had day jobs, often in computing, to pay the bills and devoted hours of their time and a lot of their own money to keep the bulletin board system going.

Though John did his sysop work for the love of computing, he believed there had to be a business idea somewhere in all this activity. So he made a bold choice: he decided to give his virus software away for free—perhaps one of the first Internet pioneers to do so while having an ultimate money-making purpose in mind. John's idea was that once he had five or ten million people using his free software, he would ask them to pay for upgrades.

It was a brilliant idea, all the more so because at first glance it seemed to fly in the face of conventional business wisdom. It was so good that other software companies—Netscape being the most obvious example—used it successfully as well.

John distributed his virus protection software through his networked bulletin boards. This led to an unexpected boon: many users took John's downloaded software and installed it on their corporate networks at work. Though John's original idea was to distribute to individuals, his software soon ended up on most computers that were networked in offices.

Around this time, software companies—Microsoft and Lotus, for example—began suing corporations for stealing software or copying it without paying for it. Because these lawsuits led to bad publicity and large settlements, most corporations began trying to head off trouble by auditing the software they had on their corporate networks. All over America, companies began to discover hundreds of copies of John's virus protection software—software for which they had failed to pay a cent. Company managers panicked—this did not look good at all. So they called John and asked how much he wanted for his software.

Imagine suddenly getting dozens of calls from people unexpectedly offering you money. It must have been dizzying, but John was smart about his response. He charged them a fairly low fee for a year's license to use his software, as opposed to a one-time fee for permanent ownership like most software products. The next year he called them (or, frequently, they called him) to renew these licenses, and he increased the price by a certain percentage. Later he began selling multiyear contracts to save the companies the hassle of contacting him every year. It was an incredible scenario: John had initially given away his product for free. Now he just sat back, took phone calls, and told people how much to make out the check for. His costs were zero and his revenue was soaring.

I met John when he was ready to take his company public. I had never seen anything like it. The operating margin—that is, the profit of his company after all expenses except taxes—was around 80 percent. I had seen profitable companies before—after all, I helped take Microsoft public—but nothing like this. It was astonishing. And not only that, but his revenues were more than doubling every year.

When I met with John one day at his company, he perfectly illustrated just how unusual his whole setup was. As we sat in a meeting room discussing the proposed IPO, John asked me to walk into the next room with him so I could observe the product launch of an upgraded version of his software. Having been in the server rooms of many large and powerful personal computer companies, I was expecting racks of computers and maybe ten programmers hustling about. Instead, one lone server stood in the middle of the room. "Computers are so powerful these days," said John. "We just don't need that much hardware."

Then he reached over and pressed a single button on the computer. "That's our product launch," he said. The upgraded software was now available on that one server. In an instant, thousands of users began "hitting" the server to download it.

This was fundamentally different from any company that I had ever seen before: John was just way ahead of the pack. Remember, this was 1992—there probably wasn't a single investor who knew what the Internet was. As the investment banker taking John public, I had to be able to help explain this phenomenon. Luckily, John's beautifully simple setup and idea made that task easier.

The offering was successful. John's company has turned into the very powerful company called Network Associates, which today has a market capitalization of $2.6 billion. The clear lesson? When it comes to business models, it's best to keep an open mind. As John's example shows, creativity is often rewarded.

Chapter 20

How Do I Get
from Here to There?

There's one critical component of the business model that entrepreneurs generally fail to consider until it's too late: the distribution model, or how exactly you plan to sell your product or service. Oh, entrepreneurs are able to figure out the target customer just fine. It's the problem of getting the product to the customer in an economically efficient way that suffers from neglect.

Kevin R. was the CEO of an IVP company. We, along with another leading venture capital firm, had invested in the company in 1995, early in the life of the commercial Internet. Kevin was a great CEO, an incredibly charismatic leader and salesman who had been a successful entrepreneur in a large firm. We had recruited him shortly after investing in the technical founders.

We were excited about this company's opportunity. It was poised to solve one of the most nagging problems facing small offices: how to easily set up and use an office network with Internet access. This was a challenge for all offices, but even more so for smaller offices, as they usually lacked the administrative or technical help to get the job done.

The company had a terrific idea: we would provide an easy-to-use and easy-to-install server that had all the prepackaged services needed to get a dozen users up on the Net. These services included, among other things, a preconfigured relationship with an ISP (Internet service provider), electronic mail, and a plug-and-play network. Just plug in a few servers and voilá! The customer has an instant Internet network. We at IVP loved it so much that we even wanted to use it in our own offices.

The press reaction to our company's product was very good. The company was able to raise millions at a high valuation. Kevin had his troops ready to roll. There was just one small problem—we lacked an efficient distribution model.

The company had decided to address the SOHO (small office home office) market, a market composed of independent consultants, salespeople who work out of their homes, and small businesses. There were thousands of these types of businesses in the United States, and the company's product was perfect for them.

The problem cropped up in trying to reach them: there was no effective distribution channel to this market. Most of the vendors providing to small businesses were large American or Japanese manufacturers—selling phones, printers, copying machines, etc.—with retail locations, or relationships with retail locations, across the country. These companies spent enormous sums on television and print advertising to drive their target customers into these retail locations. They could afford to. But large-scale national advertising is just not economically feasible for a start-up. Besides, our company had no retail locations and had not developed relationships with retailers.

Kevin was not a great salesman for nothing. He resolved to crack this nut. He first tried to get the ISPs to help sell the product—it was, after all, in their interest to sign up as many small business users as possible. What Kevin discovered after the fact was that, as a relatively new Internet phenomenon, the ISPs were overtaxed simply trying to keep up with user demand for their services. Selling to and supporting customers was a novel idea, and one that they really could not implement.

But Kevin didn't give up. He tried a second strategy: partnering with companies that were making a major effort to sell to the SOHO market. For a year, Kevin worked to sign up dozens of these relationships. This worked slightly better than focusing on the ISPs, but sales were still not taking off. The problem was that salespeople in the retail locations tended to sell products with which they were most familiar. Internet networking products didn't fit into that category, and training a scattered sales force that didn't even belong to his company was not really feasible.

By the second year, Kevin was beginning to get very frustrated. He had a great product, a defined need, a target customer ready and willing to buy, plenty of money with which to execute, and even very favorable product reviews. But sales were ramping slowly.

The lessons from Kevin's experience should be quite clear: Figure out early how you will reach your target customer. Ask yourself the following questions:

- Does a channel exist?
- Is your company equipped to utilize that channel?
- Can you make money using that channel?
- If there is an intermediary or distributor, can the intermediary or distributor make reasonable margins too?
- How does your target customer find out about your product or service?
- Does your company have the funds to reach such a customer?
- Has any other company been successful selling to your target customer through that distribution channel?
- Are you like that company (your company's economics or business model) or completely different?

Even if you plan to use the Internet as your method of customer acquisition—like the many electronic commerce companies selling drugs, cosmetics, or other merchandise online today—you still need to examine the overall economics of your channel. You need to ask yourself questions such as how the costs of shipping and fulfillment will affect the total price and decision to buy by the consumer. And if you are targeting a large but fragmented market on the Internet, such as the small business user, you still need a viable and cost-effective way to identify and reach your target customer.

Most importantly, don't start really spending money until you can answer at least some of these questions satisfactorily. Many a company has run onto the rocks in trying to solve its distribution channel issues; you need to make sure you know how to get from here to there.

Chapter 21

Is Your Business Model "Faster, Better, Cheaper" or "Brave New World"?

In Internet companies, the business model—a blueprint for how you're going to make money—is probably the single most important element. In the beginning of the Internet investment era in 1994, we at IVP discovered there were two radically different business models with which we needed to evaluate an investment.

Those two models are (1) "Faster, Better, Cheaper" and (2) "Brave New World." We first arrived at the notion of these models when we struggled with choosing which Internet companies to back. Some companies' risk was difficult to assess, because their business models were unclear: It was not at all apparent that these companies had any clear path to making money. This was a new notion for us, and it threatened to stall our foray into Internet investing.

How, for example, were we to compare investing in Excite (then known as Architext), a starving crew of Stanford graduates with a new, untested idea for a search business, with, for example, investing in a Gigabit Ethernet hardware company, an area where IVP had made lots of money in the past? The businesses were so different that we couldn't compare them. So we came up with these two categories of investment to help us compare apples to apples in assessing companies' risk profiles.

We defined "Faster, Better, Cheaper" as businesses where the business model was already clear and proven—it had been done before. Generally, these were technology companies where improvements came in cost or performance—for example, a company aimed to provide an existing product at, say, ten times the performance. The customers and the sales channels for such a product were clear and already defined, and the management team needed to have performed well in a similar business.

The costs for launching a "Faster, Better, Cheaper" business were pretty clear. And usually these companies' customers were businesses rather than consumers, at least initially. The risk in a "Faster, Better, Cheaper" investment was usually a technology risk, something that could be tested in a laboratory, which meant that the costs of the investment—until the time you knew it might be a success—were generally low and relatively controllable. Total investment for the life of the company might be in the $10 to $20 million range.

"Brave New World" investing was a whole different kettle of fish. "Brave New World" companies had no clear business models and no established sales channels. The management had no experience in the area—because nobody had experience in the area. The business had simply not existed before. How to make money was usually based on a supposition, such as advertising or subscription revenues on the Net (one of which bore out while the other flopped).

The risk in a "Brave New World" company was a market risk, something that, unlike the advance lab testing of a technology risk, could only be tested in the market. This meant that the costs of the investment—until you knew that it might be a success—were relatively large. And this was particularly true if the target market were consumers. The total cost of investment might range from $30 to $100 million, depending on how quickly your company caught on. Several of these

"Brave New World" companies were acquired in early stages by larger companies—Web TV by Microsoft, for example—so the true cost of investment to roll out the business in the market might be hidden under the mantle of a larger company.

TiVo was a good example of a "Brave New World" investment. Two managers out of Silicon Graphics, a computer technology company, founded TiVo. Both founders had been involved in early consumer trials in Orlando, Florida, of Silicon Graphics's interactive television system, a system many thought would revolutionize the way we watch TV. "Interactive television" at that time referred to video on demand: through the use of a special cable system, a customer could choose any video to watch at any time. No more trudging down to the video store! It would be right there in your TV.

But the trials had shown the product to be a dismal failure. Interactive TV, it seemed, cost too much and gave too little back to the consumer. People just didn't want to pay for it, as it didn't seem worth the cost. The founders of TiVo knew they had a lot to learn from those trials.

TiVo's product was a service called "personalized television." Basically, the company provided a box (generally sold by large consumer product partners) with storage capacity for shows on it, which the customer then hooked up to his or her TV. For a monthly fee, and using the shows the box could store, the customer could then create a personalized TV schedule, choosing what shows he or she wanted to watch, and in what order. This provided a clear benefit to advertisers: they could target advertising to a customer based on his or her demographics and preferences.

It was a novel idea, but completely unproven. If anything, the failure of Silicon Graphics's foray into interactive television might steer an investor away from this opportunity. And by any traditional evaluative standard—through the lens of "Faster, Better, Cheaper"—investing in this company was far too risky a venture.

When we analyzed it through the lens of "Brave New World," however, the potential reward seemed to outweigh the risk. We decided to invest. TiVo is still in the early stages of creating personalized television, so although it does appear that consumers are interested in these kinds of services, it's still too early to tell whether it will succeed. But in an investment climate where you must bet big to win big, our "Brave New World" framework allowed us to take the chance.

The lesson is this: Entrepreneurs should have a framework that allows them to make the same kinds of risk/reward calibrations that venture investors make each and every day. Only weighing the risk from the reward perspective will allow a founder or CEO to embark on a risky course knowing that the end result is worth the effort.

Chapter 22

Don't Let Your Mouth Make a Promise That Your Ass Can't Keep

By just about anyone's standards, Bill Gates is enormously successful. He is the richest man in the world. His and Microsoft's names are synonymous with software, technology, and the information age.

What most people don't realize is that Bill attempts to guarantee a pattern of continued success by very carefully managing other people's expectations. This became clear to me from a conversation I had with him shortly after Microsoft had gone public.

Bill called me late one night in the fall of 1986 to find out why Microsoft's stock price had spiked so high in such a short time. I told him that there was no one specific answer. Analysts at the time were recommending the stock and investors just liked the story. I kidded him about becoming a billionaire if this surge in the stock price continued. His net worth was about $350 million at the time of the IPO.

Bill seemed fairly disturbed by the prospect of achieving a personal net worth of a billion dollars. I was puzzled. "Wasn't this a great achievement," I asked, "a billionaire in less than a year?"

He replied that the accomplishment was great, just too soon. He worried aloud about investors' expectations of Microsoft and of him. He was concerned about his ability to meet such high expectations.

Sure, a billion-dollar net worth would be desirable in a few years when Microsoft had grown and prospered, but at this stage he viewed it as a liability.

This type of thinking was repeated at Microsoft's analyst presentations. Microsoft would lay out the reasons for declining growth in the worldwide PC market. Based on this slowing of PC growth, Bill would say, "Don't count on Microsoft doing as well this year as last year." The first time this managing of expectations happened at an analysts' conference, Wall Street was shocked, estimates were lowered, and the stock price plummeted. Naturally, Microsoft had its best year ever. After a few years of this Chicken Little type of behavior, Wall Street wised up and ignored Microsoft's gloomy prognostications.

Budding entrepreneurs should pay attention to this lesson. Under-promise and overdeliver. Part of successfully meeting expectations is to skillfully manage those expectations. In other words, "Don't let your mouth make a promise that your ass can't keep." Observe this rule with everybody, whether customers, investors, or employees.

Chapter 23

What Does "Burn Rate" Mean?

When you walk into the lobby of our office on Sand Hill Road, the first thing you see, hanging on the wall to your left, is an enormous, crumpled, burned-at-the-edges replica of a $1,000 bill. Grover Cleveland gazes out placidly from the center of the ravaged bill, which is a good four feet by ten feet in size.

This piece of art, entitled *The Burn Rate,* has been hanging on our wall for years. A small card placed next to the work defines "burn rate": "In the venture capital industry, in a company that has not as yet reached cash flow break-even, the burn rate is usually defined as the amount of capital consumed each month expressed in thousands of dollars. As such, it becomes the critical barometer by which a 'start-up' company's progress is measured." Burn rate is a fixed cost structure out ahead of revenues.

We have this piece of art—and the attendant explanation—in the lobby for a reason. Entrepreneurs can hardly miss it when they come in, and what better way to remind them that they have a limited time and a limited quantity of money with which to achieve their dreams? Burn rate defines that time limit. It's a notion unique to venture capital—for where else (and how else) in the world would investors build and sustain companies that may have no near-term model for profitability?

There is another notion that is starting to become critical in these Internet times: the considerable funds needed to launch large national consumer brands. Although they are variable rather than fixed, these marketing expenses (such as for television advertising or marketing promotions) are not really optional in making a consumer company successful. The company that brought this concept home to me was Purple Moon Media.

Purple Moon was an exciting, swing-for-the-fences investment IVP made in the fall of 1997. It was a software and media company spun out of Interval Research, a research center founded by Paul Allen. Paul, who cofounded Microsoft with Bill Gates back in 1975, is a big bear of a man with a very keen sense of humor and a generous spirit. In the 1980s he endured a frightening battle with Hodgkin's disease, which led him to discover a true zest for life. Though he's one of the smartest people I've ever met (Bill Gates once told me he valued Paul's friendship in part because Paul could explain almost anything Bill wanted to know), he's a low-reacting, somewhat reserved kind of guy, which has contributed to an undeserved reputation of being shy.

Paul was now a billionaire many times over, and he spent a lot of his time and money on the things that interested him: the Portland Trail Blazers basketball team, the Experience Music Project (a Jimi Hendrix museum), a Shakespeare theater, the Seattle Seahawks football team. But these weren't the only types of investments he made. He also helped start or made investments in a number of "Brave New World" Internet companies, such as America Online and Starwave.

Paul believed that technology companies were not able to make basic investments in technology research, as they were forced to be focused on near-term profits. So he founded a lab called Interval Research Corp. with my husband, David Liddle, who was a former researcher for Xerox PARC (Palo Alto Research Center). Xerox PARC, the research arm of the electronics behemoth, was legendary for creating many of the revolutionary products in the personal computer industry, now-ubiquitous products like the graphical user interface, the laser printer, and the mouse.

Interval Research is Paul Allen's 1990s version of Xerox PARC. It performs basic technology research in purely consumer areas, and out of that research it attempts to create and build companies.

Purple Moon was one such spinout company. The original research question that Interval had investigated with Purple Moon was: "Why don't girls use computers?" It was obvious that somewhere after about the age of seven, boys moved on to Nintendo and a lifetime of comfort with technology while girls stayed with Barbie and were left out in the technological cold. Interval questioned whether this made sense. Did girls intrinsically hate computers and video game machines? Or was there something wrong with what girls were being offered?

After several years of research, Interval concluded that there was something wrong with what girls were being offered. In fact, Interval discovered that girls found video games just plain dull.

This discovery led to the creation of a content company to create characters and stories for girls for personal computers and the Internet. The company was called Purple Moon and it was cool. It was cool from the first day it was launched and it stayed that way. Purple Moon resonated with my soul. On one hand, I worried about the company, because focusing on content was, after all, risky; on the other hand, the girls market seemed huge and untapped. As it turned out, the idea for Purple Moon was right—there was a big opportunity and the company was in the right place at the right time to capitalize on it. We would discover other problems later.

Nancy Deyo, the CEO of Purple Moon, was a smart, savvy woman who worked all the time. She never let a thing drop through the cracks and she was always prepared. Nancy was a first-time CEO; her job experience prior to Purple Moon was as marketing executive in a variety of companies, including—like Scott Cook of Intuit and Steven Ballmer, president of Microsoft—at Procter and Gamble.

Purple Moon had a fairly large charter. It wanted to be the Disney of the 1990s—meaning, to follow the Disney model of creating popular characters—but for girls only. Purple Moon wanted to create licensable characters that would appeal to girls—characters like Rockett, a besneakered, art-loving everygirl; Darnetta, a dreadlocked peanut-butter-hating photographer; and Dana, a tomboyish redhead—but using PCs rather than movies as the medium to launch the characters. The plan was for Purple Moon to first launch the stories and characters in CD form, then license them for a television show and a book deal and build a Web site around the characters. The Web site would have corporate sponsors interested in the girls market and would sell products and services—electronic commerce.

The launch of the company's first products hit the market like a bombshell. Customers loved the products, as did the press, which kept the company in the news. Purple Moon achieved revenue of almost $5 million in its first quarter of shipping product. Later that year, Nancy signed a book deal and was lining up both a television show and a Web publishing partnership with a major television studio. And the Web site was a huge success, with several hundred thousand visitors daily and many thousands of postcard e-mails sent from fans to the Purple Moon characters.

Purple Moon was blistering hot. Everything was in place; the hype, the momentum, the team, the product.

But there were two serious problems. One was the CD-ROM market itself, and the other was the need to spend so heavily on marketing and promotions to create and support a national consumer brand.

In the mid-1990s, when Interval Research undertook the initial research for the Purple Moon concept and the company was first started, CD-ROM companies were all the rage. Not too long afterward, after losing a lot of money on a variety of CD-ROM companies, the financial community started avoiding investments in this area.

The second problem was that the cost of launching and sustaining a national consumer retail CD-ROM brand had increased in the interim years by about four times. This was partially due to the number of brands on the market. Critical mass revenue for Purple Moon had increased from $25 million to $100 million. We were prepared for national launch costs of about $20 million, but we were unprepared for how much it cost to sustain a national CD-ROM brand. The company's Web revenues from sponsorship and e-commerce, while interesting and innovative, were just not enough to replace the CD-ROM revenue and allow us to become a pure Web company.

Because of all the promotions necessary to sustain a successful national consumer brand, Purple Moon was spending almost $2 million a month. This is a daunting number—and when the company had to cut revenue projections in mid-1998, due to softness in the CD retail market, it came into play even more. Purple Moon, which had been in fairly serious discussions with a number of strategic partners, needed another $30 million to cash flow breakeven. And nearly $20 million had already been invested in the company.

We decided to look for a larger partner for the company that could spend the necessary dollars on the brand. Eventually, after officially going out of business, Purple Moon was sold to Mattel Media, which owned the competing Barbie brand.

The lesson in Purple Moon is *not* that you need to always keep expenses low. In some businesses, including most Internet consumer businesses, that notion is slow death. Your company would never build the necessary marketing presence to be successful. That was absolutely the case with Purple Moon.

I believe our problem was the changing CD-ROM market, which both raised our expenses and caused potential new financial investors to avoid us. So I guess the lesson would be to try and make sure—if you require large sums to support marketing or promotions—that the area will likely be perceived as "hot" for some time to come so that the necessary funds will be forthcoming.

Venture Capitalists

Chapter 24

The Five Stages of Every Venture Capital Deal

When an entrepreneur has hatched an idea, identified a market, and worked up a business plan, it's time to find some money and get the new company rolling. Here's where the venture capitalists come in.

Venture capital deals are as different as the people, companies, and ideas that are involved in them. But they do have one thing in common: the five stages.

- Initial pitch
- Follow-up meetings
- Due diligence
- Partner meeting pitch
- Deal negotiation and close

The Initial Pitch

The first and most critical meeting is the initial pitch. If you don't succeed here, you're not going to get any further.

Given how important this pitch is, it's surprising how many entrepreneurs go into it without being prepared. Many come, for example, without a Powerpoint presentation—they come in as though they're stopping in for a chat. This is a serious mistake. You generally have one hour to win a venture capitalist's attention: you need to have prepared a crisp oral presentation in advance, preferably with slides and visuals, to convey all the pertinent information and still leave time for questions. As the actress Ruth Gordon once said, "The best impromptu speeches are the ones written well in advance."

If a venture capitalist prefers not to hear a presentation, he or she will say so. But it's by far the most effective use of limited time to explain an idea. If I were an entrepreneur, I would insist on doing one if the venture capitalist gives any choice in the matter.

There are, of course, cases in which entrepreneurs get investments without having prepared presentations. We have funded companies after meeting technologists who have none of the essential elements—no market presentation, no clear-cut idea of product or competition. But that approach only works if you're a brilliant technologist with a brilliant idea. For the rest of us mere mortals, some kind of structure or framework helps the venture capitalist crystallize the idea and helps us determine how well you think.

The presentation should include the following:

- A vision statement
- A description of the market opportunity and growth potential
- Background information on the management team
- A description of the product and/or its technology
- A business model that includes a distribution model
- A description of the competition
- How much money needs to be raised and a rough estimate of cash flow
- Key variables for success

The entrepreneur should come alone or with one other member of the management team (if there is another member). Most importantly, he or she should be prepared to answer any questions and be ready to give the logic behind an answer as well as the answer itself.

If this all sounds very structured, believe me, it's not. It's a free-form chance to float your idea for the venture capitalist, who will be trying to assess a number of things—whether the idea is good, whether the market is promising, even whether there is any chemistry between you and him or her. Based on all these factors, the venture capitalist will decide whether to proceed to the next step:

The Follow-up Meeting

If the venture capitalist sees potential in an idea or company, he or she will schedule a follow-up meeting between the entrepreneur and several partners. Part of the purpose of this meeting is for that first partner to get a second (or third or fourth) opinion about the potential investment. There may even be several of these meetings. Often the other partners will back up the impression of the initial partner, but sometimes they will express reservations about the idea, the entrepreneur, or both. If these reservations are serious enough, they can gut the entrepreneur's chances even though the initial partner was interested.

Due Diligence

During the follow-up meetings, the partners begin a due diligence process, which basically means they gather information to assess the founders, the market opportunity, the technology, and the competition. Due diligence can take many forms. For example, customer due diligence (which is the most important kind of due diligence) involves talking to potential customers to gauge interest in the product or service. IVP, like many partnerships, sends entrepreneurs to meet with executives or employees in our own portfolio companies. Because we've worked with these people in building their companies, we know and understand their thinking and trust their technical judgment. These meetings are completely confidential—these entrepreneurs don't reveal information given to them. We make sure that there is no competitive overlap. Their assessments are an important element in helping us to decide whether to fund a new company.

Venture capitalists will ask entrepreneurs for references—names of colleagues, partners, and customers we can call. We venture capitalists do call these references, but we also dig a little deeper and do "outside" due diligence—asking others about you and talking to your competitors or former employers or employees. This is just part of the process, a standard way for us to get as much information as we can.

I once tracked down a former founder of an entrepreneur's company in the process of doing due diligence. The entrepreneur hadn't listed him as a reference, but I felt he would have relevant insight. He gave the entrepreneur a pretty good review. But later, the entrepreneur was upset that I had talked to his company's former founder. Venture capitalists try as soon as possible to go beyond the reference list that you provide—so don't be surprised if we talk to a variety of people.

Sometimes we meet with the entrepreneurs to go over what we've discovered—meetings that can involve critiques of the idea or company. Though this can be uncomfortable, we're trying to work through any problems with the deal. Understand that criticism is aimed at being constructive, not at finding a reason not to invest. Some of the most valuable exchanges in developing the company can occur at this point in the process.

If at any point in the process the partner stops meeting with or calling the entrepreneur, it is in all probability a sign that we are cooling on the deal. Venture capitalists are busy, but if we're interested in working with you, we'll find time to call. This is not meant to be a slight; it's just that so many things are happening at once, and only a few companies can get priority attention at any given time. If we do have the time, we will make a point of calling the entrepreneur and giving the reasons for not investing.

This is maddening to entrepreneurs who think they're about to be funded, only to find out that interest in their company had waned a while back. My advice is that entrepreneurs who aren't getting calls back or requests for more meetings should probably move on and look for other opportunities.

The Partner Meeting Pitch

The partner meeting pitch is one of the last hurdles. In most venture capital firms, the full partnership (or a certain subset of it) must gather and review a deal before it's approved. The entrepreneur will be asked to present in front of the partnership and answer questions.

There are a few really important things for entrepreneurs to keep in mind for this presentation. The first and most important is to answer the questions directly and succinctly. Entrepreneurs often have so much to say, and so much eagerness to get it all out, that they digress. Remember, you can lose the partnership—and more—between the beginning and end of a meandering answer. Time is critical: You generally have one hour to get through your presentation and answer any questions.

In the interest of time, only one or two entrepreneurs need make the actual presentation, though it's good for the top members of the management team—marketing, development, and sales—to come along for the meeting. The point of this meeting is to answer questions; it does no one any good if a lot of time is wasted having team members hop up and down to make bits of a presentation.

Deal Negotiation

If the partner pitch goes well, then the entrepreneur moves to the final stage, deal negotiation. This part is usually the most confusing to the entrepreneur; getting a good attorney, who can offer useful advice about similar deals and the valuations they garnered, is a smart move.

Valuation—determining how much the idea and company are worth—is the most critical aspect of the negotiation, because it sets the stage for deciding how the ownership of the company will be divided up after the initial financing. Generally, the company will be divided among three owners: the founders, the future employees (also called the employee pool), and the venture capitalists. There are no hard-and-fast rules, but we venture capitalists are most sensitive to our ownership and to that of the future employee pool.

Many partnerships have very strict rules about how much the firm must own before the partner can agree to sit on the board of directors. (This is known as an "active investment." If an investment doesn't include a board seat, it's known as a "passive investment.") Target ownership for an active investment is approximately 25 percent (for a passive investment, the figure is around 10 percent). These percentages can be higher if the company requires a lot of work, such as help in hiring a new management team.

At this point, entrepreneurs are sometimes dealing with several venture capital firms, some of which may be offering a higher valuation than others. Though it's tempting to go with the firm offering the highest valuation, we recommend that entrepreneurs optimize on picking a great partner, not just on price. The goal is to work with a venture capital partner who will help you build a great company, not just one who will agree to give you the highest valuation. A smaller piece of a large pie is usually worth more than a larger piece of a small pie.

Before choosing, entrepreneurs are well advised to do their own due diligence, by calling the founders and management of the venture capitalist's portfolio companies and asking about the firm's philosophy. Are they supportive in troubled times or do they cut and run? Does the partner have real time to give you? Has he or she worked hard for his or her portfolio companies? This is one of the biggest decisions a fledgling company will make; it's a mistake to scrimp on the time needed to come to the right choice.

Once an agreement is made with a venture capital firm, the first five stages are done. Now comes the most exciting stage of all: building a great company and making lots of money for the entrepreneurs and investors.

Chapter 25

Think of Us As Partners

I confess; I was worried. John N., the CEO of one of our Internet companies, had called to fill me in on a conversation he'd just had with one of the founders of a company I was hoping to invest in. The founder had called John to do some background checking on us. This was a good thing: the relationship between venture capitalists and founders is a partnership, and I always encourage them to do the same kind of due diligence homework on us as we do on them.

But John wasn't calling as a simple courtesy. He wanted to warn me against making an investment in this particular company. During his conversation with one of the founders, John detected a lot of suspicion and mistrust about the role venture capitalists play in developing companies. In particular, it seemed that the founder and his colleagues believed that venture capitalists were out to get rid of them—by stealing their company out from under them. "Do the venture capitalists run your company?" the founder had asked John. "Do they control your board of directors? Have they tried to grab back your stock?"

As I listened to John, I felt a familiar sinking feeling. The relationship between founders and venture capitalists is variable. Before an investment is agreed on, we start out in a naturally somewhat antagonistic position: we're negotiating terms, and each side is trying to get a fair deal. But once the investment is agreed on, we are instantly on the same side, with the same goal: building a great company.

It's kind of like negotiating a prenuptial agreement. On the one hand, you're discussing the great future relationship that lies ahead. But on the other hand, you're already discussing the terms of the divorce. It's a tricky negotiation, one that requires a certain amount of trust in order not to collapse. If the founders mistrust the investors, the difficult business of starting a company is made much more difficult unnecessarily. And that mistrust can become downright corrosive when things get tougher down the road.

These founders were afraid. They feared we would take over, fire them, and strip them of the results of their hard work. Their fear was understandable—it comes from hearing horror stories and from inexperience with the process. Our firm believes that the only way to work with a company is in a true spirit of partnership—that without the cooperation and support of the founders, the company usually cannot succeed. The best way to get over fear is to talk to the companies that the venture capitalists have backed. These entrepreneurs have been in a partnership with venture capitalists, and they can explain the partnership's philosophy.

But these founders decided to build in their own safeguards: they asked for a number of unusual guarantees. They might have thought this was a perfect solution, but in reality it was shortsighted. All the built-in guarantees completely undermined the authority of the CEO the founders had recruited to manage the company. Taking away the CEO's authority to make consequential hiring and firing decisions would not only damage morale, but would also foster grudges against the founders for their excessive degree of protection.

When you're negotiating a deal, it's very easy to get wrapped up in it and not see the forest for the trees. Because he wasn't a participant, John was able to take a more objective view than me—and he was clearly worried about the founder's tone. John's call really brought the problem into sharp relief.

The founders' phone call to John and his subsequent call to me tell you everything you need to know about the extremes of trust and mistrust among founders, managers, and venture capitalists. The very fact that John, a CEO of one of our companies, called to let me know about his conversation—and to offer his candid opinion about it—is an illustration of the ideal partner-type relationship. He wanted to help us as we considered this investment decision, and we trusted his judgment.

We did ultimately agree to all the founders' demands concerning salary guarantees and vesting. We would not ordinarily have agreed to this, but we liked what the company was doing. But the founders were uncomfortable with other terms, terms that, in only a few very defined and narrow cases, put the company's interests, rather than the founders' personal interests, first.

The CEO really wanted to do a deal, but he couldn't convince the founders to concede enough points. The more we negotiated, the clearer it became that the founders' mistrust of venture capitalists was going to scuttle any hopes of working fruitfully together. In the end, we did not invest in the company.

The key points to remember:

1. *Relationships drive the business process.*
2. *It's not possible to contractually anticipate and protect against every risk in business relationship.* Business partnerships are generally created to realize the upside, not to protect against the downside.
3. *Approaching a partnership in a totally contractual vein usually results in no partnership—or one so constrained that little comes of it.* Trust and judgment about people and their intentions is a vital part of business negotiation. That's why lawyers are not generally great businessmen: they are paid to anticipate the worst.

Venture capitalists, on the other hand, anticipate the best. View us as partners, rather than as competitors or antagonists. After all, in the end your goal is exactly the same as ours: the success of your company.

Chapter 26

Feedback Is a Buying Sign

Listening is an art. Listening when someone gives you advice you don't want to hear is an even finer art. And listening to advice you don't want to hear and then acting on it is the highest art form of all.

Listening is tough for entrepreneurs. To be a successful founder, you must have enough confidence in yourself and your idea to forge ahead when others are less convinced of its merits than you are. If you are willing to change or even dump your idea based on whatever someone else tells you, it brings into question how solid your idea—and your confidence in it—was in the first place.

But being confident in your idea is not the same as being unwilling to listen to feedback or advice about it. After all, feedback from potential investors is a good thing. It shows that they're interested and are looking for ways to make the company successful. The ability of an entrepreneur to really listen to and consider suggestions about his or her idea is a sign of confidence in that idea.

The longer we sat across the table from Patrick N., the founder and CEO of a start-up company we were considering investing in, the more we realized that he had not really listened to our issues. In a flurry of e-mails prior to this meeting—the latest in a long series of meetings—my partner and I had outlined for Patrick the major issues still standing in the way of our investment in his company. Patrick had brought in his management team to address those issues.

It was late at night, well after dinnertime. My fellow partner Pete Thomas and I met with four or five of the company's senior executives in our largest conference room. It was the end of a very busy day, and we were tired. We had given lots of feedback to this company. The purpose of this meeting was to get some of our very specific questions answered, and we were excited about moving things forward.

The vice president of sales opened the meeting with a presentation: a long, slow, and detailed repetition of all our prior discussions. Ostensibly this presentation was supposed to answer our questions. But all the vice president was telling us was things we already knew.

As the vice president continued, I glanced over at Pete. He's our most technically oriented partner, a former Intel employee who loves doing unusual and technical "swing-for-the-fences" deals. Pete's a low-reactor kind of guy, but there's a lot going on behind his placid features. All I saw on his face was patient attention to the presentation, but he told me afterward that he was thinking the same thing: "He's about to get to the important part. He's bound to get to the important part soon." Trouble was, he never did. An hour later, the vice president finished his presentation, and we still hadn't moved the discussion forward.

Patrick's company was a "Brave New World" company with a simple, effective idea for bridging the gap between TV and Internet use. Using Patrick's software and a specially designed remote control, TV viewers could "capture" one of the increasingly ubiquitous URLs (such as NBA.com) shown in television advertisements. Then, using an Internet-enabled television, the viewer could use the captured URL to go directly to a Web site, which immediately provided more advertiser information about that specific product.

We thought the idea of a service to bridge television and the Internet was pretty interesting. The viewer had the benefit of instantly getting more information on a product; the advertiser could provide more information on a product to a clearly interested consumer; and the networks could keep the viewer on their captive site for a longer period of time, thereby garnering more advertising dollars.

As good as the idea seemed, Patrick had been trying unsuccessfully to get venture financing for more than a year. He had made countless presentations. He had even borrowed against his home to meet payroll—and the note was due in two weeks. His idea was good, the timing was clearly right, and Patrick was eager to get started. But after many meetings and many hours spent discussing the company's strategy, I now knew part of the reason why Patrick had been unsuccessful in getting anyone to back him. It was because he couldn't—or wouldn't—listen and respond to the specific questions we raised.

The idea had some fundamental problems, two of which were particularly pressing. First, Patrick needed distribution partnerships to get the special remote controls his product required into the hands of the viewing audience. Distribution is a key part of any business model, and its failure can sabotage a good business idea. Patrick's other solution to getting the remotes to his audience was to rely upon another start-up company that was in the business of making innovative new remotes. Relying upon another start-up company for your company's product to succeed is dangerous. The more dominoes that have to fall, the more uncertain the outcome becomes.

As we sat across the table from Patrick, the disconnect between our thinking and his was clear. He was already focusing on all the great data that could be collected with his product rather than on the critical prior step of how to get working devices to consumers easily and cheaply.

We questioned Patrick repeatedly on these points. His answers were varied but somewhat vague. His attitude seemed to be: Just give me the money, let me do what I think is right, and then I will focus on your concerns.

As I looked at Patrick, I felt sympathy for him. He looked tired. His clothes were hanging on him as though he'd lost weight. He looked as if the year that he had spent trying to convince potential investors had taken its toll, both physically and emotionally. Mortgaging your house to meet payroll is usually the type of bold behavior that helps an entrepreneur win. But maybe, I thought as I looked at his slumping frame, Patrick had sacrificed too much for too long.

Not surprisingly, we didn't back Patrick's company, even though we were very interested in investing in the type of company he was proposing. Granted, there were still many issues to work through, competitive and otherwise, that may have prevented us from investing—but his attitude made going any further impossible.

The fine art of listening—really listening—and then trying to respond will serve an entrepreneur well in any business situation. If an entrepreneur cannot engage in a real discussion and listen carefully to our issues, how can he hope to do so with employees, other partners, or customers? If he shows himself incapable of absorbing input and making decisions based on more, rather than less, information, how can he hope to create a successful company?

Chapter 27

Seeing Shows That Aren't in TV Guide

We have nothing but admiration for the entrepreneurs who come and present their ideas in initial pitches to us venture capitalists every day. It must be difficult to sketch the blueprint of your dream to a dispassionate observer. No matter how polite the proceedings may be, it's bound to be unnerving, a fact we try to keep in mind when things don't go so well during a pitch or subsequent meetings with an entrepreneur.

As nerve-racking as it may be, your presentation to venture capitalists can make or break your company's financial future. Here are a few things for entrepreneurs to keep in mind when presenting:

- Answer directly the question put to you
- Present for no more than an hour, no matter how many questions you get—unless the partners beg you to stay and keep talking
- Make sure your demo works before you come—you don't want to be embarrassed by showing off a product that doesn't work
- Know what you want to ask for in terms of money and assistance
- No stretching the truth—you'll be found out in the end

I call this last point "seeing shows that aren't in *TV Guide*"—basically, seeing or presenting a situation as other than it really is. Sometimes people want desperately to see something that isn't really there, so they stretch or manipulate the truth. But, like the listings in *TV Guide*, what's on is what's on. And it does no one any good to spin a different, incorrect version of what that may be.

In many ways this is the most critical point to remember in your presentation. It's damaging to your cause to present us something other than the reality of your situation. You can (and should) be positive when you present, but you should also be balanced and give us the downside as well—otherwise we'll be forced to find the problems ourselves rather than having you point them out. And stretching the truth might seem a good idea in the short run, but in the end you'll be caught out, and the consequences will be worse than if you had just told the plain truth to begin with.

There are exceptions, of course, as in the story I'm about to tell about some young entrepreneurs who set an example of how not to deal with venture capitalists. They were lucky this time—their company could easily have crashed and burned, but it didn't. In less exuberant markets than we have right now, it well might have.

All but one of these founders, who were in their late twenties, had been students together at Berkeley. They were young, bright, and ambitious. These young entrepreneurs had founded a company to do Web site maintenance. Prior to meeting with us, they demonstrated their diagnostic test on our own Web site, an illustration that was impressive and highly illuminating. It gave us a real feel for what their software could do for a customer. Not only did they have a great product, they had also done a fair amount of market research, so they had a good feel for their true market potential.

I was working on this opportunity with one of our venture partners, Peter Gotcher, who was a former entrepreneur himself. In the late 1980s he founded Digidesign, a company that had successfully gone public and been sold. Peter and I were quite excited about this opportunity. All that was left was to make a few due diligence calls to the company's customers and partners, and we'd be ready to move forward.

In our last meeting with the founders, we talked a bit about their customers and partners. "We're in discussions with several portal companies, including one of the largest portal sites, to be our customers," one of them told us. This was good news. Not only was this portal a well-known and successful company, but it was one of our investments, and so it would be easier for us to call and do the due diligence. They then named a few more Web sites I was familiar with and had good contacts for. "Fabulous," I told them. "Send us the contact names and your references, and we'll start calling immediately."

Several days went by, and the references didn't arrive. Peter called to follow up. "They're on their way," the founders told us. And after a while, the references did arrive. Unfortunately, they didn't contain any of the promised high-profile Web sites as customer contacts. There were several customers listed, but none of the ones mentioned in the meeting. Peter called the founders to follow up. "Where are the contact names of the high-profile Web site customers?" he asked. "We've got the list you sent, but it doesn't have the names you promised."

"Well," one of the founders responded, "we were hoping you could help us contact them. We haven't actually started discussion with any of them yet."

This was very surprising. What was more disappointing was that the list of references they *had* sent would have been presentable (though it did lack the credibility that a top-tier customer name brings) if we hadn't been expecting the names of the big guys. In their eagerness to please us, these young founders had overreached, trying to impress us with top-tier names.

Since we liked both these guys and their idea, Peter and I asked them to come back when they had one or two of the more high-profile names on the list. The relationship had started off on the wrong foot because they overpromised and underdelivered. But what we really wanted to know was whether their company was good enough to get those top-tier names.

We didn't end up funding the company, but I later heard that another leading venture capital firm did. About a year later, a large Net company purchased them. And shortly after that, AOL purchased the Net company for $4 billion.

This story turned out well for these founders, who had a good idea and were able to execute on it. The lesson here is that most entrepreneurs have exciting stories all their own. There's no need to embellish or overpromise, to "see shows that aren't in *TV Guide*."

Entrepreneurs

Chapter 28

Five Common Mistakes
First-Time Entrepreneurs Make

To paraphrase Tolstoy, successful companies are alike, but every unsuccessful company is unsuccessful in its own way. Why? Because there are a limited number of things that can go right in an investment, but an unlimited number of things that can go wrong.

In earlier chapters, I have attempted to outline some of the biggest mistakes that first-time entrepreneurs can make, including: ramping the company before the technology is proven, overestimating the size of the market opportunity, or allowing the burn rate to control the company's destiny. The field of potential mistakes is vast and varied. Here are five of the common ones made by first-time (and sometimes second- and third-time) entrepreneurs.

Mistake #1: Hiring the Wrong Person to Fill a Key Position

Start-up companies move at the speed of light: events overtake planning, everyone is forced into playing multiple roles for the company, and there's never enough time to get things done. In that kind of atmosphere—when you want to hire people as quickly as you can—it's easy to compromise on getting the very best people, with the expectation of hiring a better person later. But the cost of this approach will only become evident to you later. And believe me, it is high.

Quick, half-baked hiring is a seductive short-term solution. Once you've gotten someone—anyone—on board, you'll feel relieved: the job is filled, a body is in place, the pressure is off. But that feeling of well-being wears off soon enough, supplanted by worry about whether your new hire can make the right decisions for the business. If he or she can't—or even if you simply aren't certain they can—you will likely be drawn in to making that person's decisions yourself, in an effort to protect your company. Then you'll be in exactly the position you were in before—except now you're carrying along an extra person and doing that work yourself.

Keep your standards high. Have patience. Find the team that you trust to help grow your company. And delegate to them to do it. You'll be further ahead at the end of the process, with much less frustration.

This advice must be somewhat modified for very fast-moving industries, such as the Internet. While you still need to keep your standards high, not making a key hire might spell the difference between success and failure. Many of my Internet investments have adapted to this situation by keeping quality standards high while relaxing a little on the breadth or depth of experience of a candidate. We might take more of a risk, by hiring someone who's less experienced but very capable and bright, with the hope that such a candidate might ultimately grow into the position.

Mistake #2: Thinking Small to Reduce Risk

I'm very familiar with this problem, for good reason. As a less seasoned venture capitalist, and in an effort not to screw up right off the mark, I've suffered from it myself. This is the inclination to go for the more conservative play, in an effort to minimize risk. But think about it: the odds are against your success anyway, regardless. And the smaller play might have just as many—albeit different—risks.

Go for it. Just make sure the reward and risk are commensurate—

that if you take on all this risk and work your tail off, the reward at the end is worth it. Making start-up companies successful on any level is just plain hard. So why not win big if you do win? This advice ties in with the earlier chapter on identifying a big market. Sometimes an entrepreneur will go after a smaller market because it appears more comprehensible or because there is less competition, but a large market opportunity can make up for a multitude of other mistakes.

Mistake #3: Telling Venture Capitalists What You Think They Want to Hear

This can be a particularly foolish thing to do, especially since you may end up obscuring the very things the venture capitalist really does want to hear.

Here's an example. An entrepreneur came to IVP with a brilliant idea. He had done his homework—done some reading, talked to a few people—and gotten information on ideas that had recently been funded. Afraid to let his idea stand on its own, he proceeded to present his idea to us as cut from the same or similar cloth as ideas that had just gotten funding, thinking that would increase his chances.

In fact, he twisted and manipulated his idea so much that it wasn't clear to us what the original notion really was. Luckily for us and for him, we spent enough time to peel back the layers and figure out what he was actually proposing. But we cannot always take that amount of time and effort. Present your idea as what it is. It will save us time, it will save you time, and your being straightforward with us will increase our desire to work with you.

Mistake #4: Believing Your Competition Is Incompetent

Paranoia has a PR problem: it's cast in a negative light, but it can also be hugely useful. In fact, it's a key characteristic common to successful entrepreneurs.

Bill Gates and Andy Grove, two of the most successful entrepreneurs in the country, are both raging paranoiacs. No matter how much market share they get, no matter how much their companies are worth, no matter how many magazine covers their faces grace, they always have their ears cocked for the rumble of competition approaching from behind.

They run their companies as though they expect at any moment they could be put out of business; it keeps them alert and focused. And that's not just an intellectual exercise. Remember IBM's domination of personal computers? Or WordStar's domination of word processing software? These companies were industry behemoths, but they were overtaken by hungrier, more aggressive companies. Remember, if you have a part of the market, there's someone out there who wants—and could well be able— to take it from you. Never underestimate the competition.

Mistake #5: Focusing Solely on the Money

It's no secret that people who start companies would like to make money from them. But if that's the sole reason an entrepreneur creates a company, a number of problems can result: focusing on short-term gains to the long-term detriment of the company, inability to motivate employees who may have a much smaller piece of the pie, or lack of an overall vision for growing the company, to name a few.

An old parable holds that you can chase a butterfly for hours and never catch it, but if you sit calmly it will alight on your shoulder. You've got to be a little more proactive than just sitting calmly in order to build a company, of course, but the basic idea holds true. If you're frenetically chasing money (as opposed to building your vision for the company), you'll likely end up with less of it in the long run.

Chapter 29

Real Entrepreneurs
Quit Their Day Jobs

Creating a technology company is not for the faint of heart. The great rewards come with even greater risks. I was reminded of this when two engineers from the research labs at Hewlett-Packard came to see me about funding their new start-up software company. The business plan wasn't bad and the two scientists were clearly experts in the security software that would form the basis for their new company. The essential missing ingredient was their attitude. Both planned to keep their day jobs at HP right up to the point of a venture capitalist like myself handing over the check to start the company.

You see the problem. If neither of these two fellows believed enough in their idea to risk even a month's worth of unemployment, why should we risk our time and our firm's millions? We chose not to fund them because they were unwilling to be bold. Boldness and calculated risk taking often spell the difference between success and failure in Silicon Valley.

Philippe Kahn, founder of Borland, is one of the best examples of what I mean by bold. He's a renaissance man, a hefty Frenchman whose wardrobe of choice is shorts and Hawaiian shirts. He's a musician, a sailor, and a pilot, and he used to go out to the airport every night to get in his plane and trace loops and other aerobatic moves in the night sky.

Philippe came to California from France and started Borland with no money, selling computer language products through groundbreaking mail-order ads. When Borland first entered the spreadsheet wars against the much more established competitors, Lotus and Microsoft, Philippe came up with the blockbuster marketing idea of allowing customers to swap their existing old spreadsheet for Borland's newer one for free. Realizing that market share was everything, Philippe was willing to lose the battle to win the war. He was a master of this kind of standout marketing—spending a tenth of what his competitors spent while attracting twice the attention.

An experience that I had with Philippe a few years ago best illustrates what I mean. My husband and I were returning home from a flying show late one night in Philippe's private plane. Philippe's flying instructor was piloting our plane while Philippe was following us in his open-cockpit aerobatics biplane. Because his antique biplane lacked the necessary instruments to fly safely in cloudy night conditions, Philippe was relying upon his instructor to help guide him.

The instructor was having a hard time giving directions to him because he couldn't identify which plane was Philippe's against a backdrop of other planes and stars. Philippe solved our problem in his normal bold and effective manner. "I will do a loop," he said, in his best parody of Inspector Clouseau. As we gazed out the plane's right window, one of the points of light pulled away from all of the others and traced a large loop in the sky. Well, after that performance, we certainly knew which plane was Philippe's. He had—as usual—managed to attract the maximum amount of attention with the least amount of time and trouble.

Philippe has continued making bold bets. His most recent start-up—Starfish Software, a company that created basic operating software for Swatch watches and Motorola pocket-size cellular phones to enable miniature, wearable computers—was just sold to Motorola for several hundred million dollars. Philippe recognized early on that size and wearability would be the major issues of computers designed strictly for consumers. He calls it "softwear"—and he bet his entire company and livelihood on this insight.

Philippe jokes that designer sneakers are his next target. One day, your shoes may adjust themselves automatically for different types of exercise. Given his knack for bold marketing, I would not put it past Philippe to program your Nikes to automatically carry you into the nearest shoe store when they need to be replaced.

Chapter 30

Five Things a CEO Should Not Say at a Board Meeting

Board of directors' meetings of early-stage companies are unique affairs. Their purpose is straightforward: to allow company management to bounce ideas off the directors, to update board members on the company's progress, and to allow everyone to work together on strategy. No hard-and-fast formula exists for board meetings; there are as many different ways to conduct them as there are CEOs who do it. Depending on how open the CEO is to soliciting and absorbing advice from the board, the meetings can range from headbangingly frustrating to remarkably productive. The environment should be one where the CEO and management team feel comfortable sharing concerns with the board.

No matter what kind of board meeting you're in though, there are five things a CEO should avoid saying:

1. "Our competitors are way behind."
2. "If that's the way the board feels, maybe you should get someone else to run the company."
3. "I know we're behind plan, but a cutback now would hurt morale."

4. "[silence]" (when what's needed is an admission that the CEO made a mistake or bad decision).
5. "I have some surprise bad news!"

"OUR COMPETITORS ARE WAY BEHIND."

Deriding (and underestimating) the competition is a common mistake for CEOs, who often believe so passionately in their own companies that they're lulled into thinking everybody else is naturally second-rate. But beware! I have heard CEOs dismiss their competition, only to be forced to eat their words at the very next board meeting when the same competitor announces a great new customer or strategic partner. You could be setting yourself up for a nasty surprise. Besides that, the board may worry about your judgment in other matters if you can't analyze the competition objectively.

"IF THAT'S THE WAY THE BOARD FEELS, MAYBE YOU SHOULD GET SOMEONE ELSE TO RUN THE COMPANY."

This is the "flounce out in a huff" scenario, a cheap stab at emotional blackmail. The message this statement sends is purely emotional, and it effectively kills rational discussion on the issues, with the result of calling into question your maturity and leadership. What's worse, it can force the very thing you fear, but for the wrong reasons. After all, you've just given the board the notion of replacing you when it might not have been under consideration at all.

"I KNOW WE'RE BEHIND PLAN, BUT A CUTBACK NOW WOULD HURT MORALE."

This is my personal favorite. The company is behind plan, in trouble, with a fixed amount of cash, possibly headed toward flameout—

but never mind that! What's important, argues the CEO, is employee morale. Never mind about what employee morale will be when the company implodes and goes out of business.

"[SILENCE]."

This is a sin of omission rather than of commission. Many CEOs find it very difficult to simply admit that they made a mistake. "I made a mistake" is not the ideal thing you want to hear from your CEO, but taking responsibility for a mistake shows a welcome maturity. If you've made a wrong decision, admit it and move on: your board of directors will respect you more for it.

"I HAVE SOME SURPRISE BAD NEWS."

The only objectionable part of this phrase is the word "surprise." There will always be ups and down with any start-up company, and one can't always predict when a deal or partnership will close. Bad news is an expected part of the game. However, the CEO must believe that the board is there to help. He or she must be ready to share concerns *early* with the board. That's what it's there for: to give advice and to act as a sounding board for the management team. If the board is unaware of potential problems until the last minute, it won't be able to help the CEO solve them. These are the problems that become "surprise" bad news.

Chapter 31

Hype Is a Double-Edged Sword

If living in Silicon Valley is like being in a bubble, hype is the oxygen we breathe inside. Hype is everywhere, fueling new companies, pushing tech stocks to dizzying heights, alternately blessing and cursing entrepreneurs and their ideas all over the Valley.

Some of the highest valuations and biggest returns I've seen in the last five years have come from companies that were initially viewed as pure hype—companies that were able to grow into more substantial businesses using the capital and fanfare generated from the surrounding buzz. The current superinflated Internet stock prices are another example of hype at work. Will the Internet change our lives? Yes. Does that mean that Internet companies that are losing money should be worth several billion dollars in market capitalization? Who knows? But hype wins out, and the ticker spits out bigger and bigger numbers.

Hype makes me squeamish. I instinctively shy away from it, believing that anything that needs to be hyped is probably not for real. This is a disadvantage to me as a venture capitalist, as hype does bring some advantages. For a little start-up company trying to stay afloat in the roiling waters of competition, it at least brings some notice. Let's face it: most start-ups fail. So it pays to have all the advantages you can get, even if the expectations hype brings may be greater than what your company can fulfill.

But beware of the negative effects hype can visit on a company's fortunes:

Waking the giant: Hype can focus the attention of larger competitors on a small company before it's prepared or able to compete with them.

Rallying the critics: All of Silicon Valley, and I mean all, yearns for the failure of overhyped companies. Everyone keeps one eye out for the slightest stumble, so they can proclaim the whole thing was air all along.

Inflating expectations: Hype causes expectations to be set very high early on in the company's life, causing anything other than tremendous success to be viewed as failure.

Waking the Giant

Go Corporation and Netscape are good examples of companies that were overhyped early on, invoking the fury of a larger competitor. Their stories differ, but there's one key similarity: both of these companies were gnats compared to their shared competitor, Microsoft.

Go had developed a pen-based operating system, a product that was expected to revolutionize the way we use computers. In the hype that built up around the company, the press needled Microsoft so much that the software giant finally introduced a competitive product aimed at swatting the gnat—putting Go out of business. Microsoft never really got serious about building its pen-based business, and a few years later its pen business and the upstart Go were both out of business.

By 1995 Netscape, one of the earliest superhyped Internet companies, was positioning itself in conjunction with Java as the next generation after Windows. Microsoft, which came late to the Internet party, was annoyed at little Netscape's positioning—and for its part, Netscape took every opportunity to shake its tiny fist in the behemoth's face. Netscape was an industry darling, and the smart little company seemed like the perfect David to whip Microsoft's cocky Goliath.

Rallying the Critics

The second drawback of hype—Silicon Valley rooting for your company's failure—is much less damaging than awakening a giant competitor. The simple fact of having competitors and observers secretly pining for your demise is not enough to cause a company to fail, but it does paint a rather large bull's-eye on your chest, and it can create extra pressure on the company.

Inflating Expectations

As a Silicon Valley executive once said to me, "There are two paths a company can follow. The first is to hype the company, have the bar set very high, and later to disappoint. The second is to proceed more quietly and then shock everyone with your progress."

The drawback of hype's creating exorbitant expectations is a serious one, and it can have a profound effect on the morale of your company's employees. Even though your company may be making normal progress, the expectations created by too much hype render normal progress as subpar. This puts even more pressure on employees in the most difficult stages of building a company, and employee defections can result. Newly public companies worry about defections as well, but for a different reason: if the bubble of skyrocketing stock prices burst, and the company's stock price becomes severely deflated, employees will stream out all available exits. In these cases, company fundamentals may be fine, but the plummeting stock price indicates otherwise.

One more thing about hype: much of Silicon Valley is naturally superstitious about success drawing the ire of the Heavens. Perhaps one reason is the strange history of the Stanford Alumni Association award, which is given each year to a successful entrepreneur-started Silicon Valley company.

The award is very carefully considered and very prestigious—not an instrument of hype—but it does bring the spotlight on companies in a concentrated way. The funny thing is that for as long as anyone can remember, many of the companies that win this award, which is presented at a fancy dinner attended by Silicon Valley glitterati, have gone on to suffer something pretty terrible befalling them in the year or so afterward. Netscape, Ascend, Intuit, Borland, Electronic Arts—all these companies won the award and suffered some difficulty shortly afterward. (To be fair, a few companies who received the award, including Cisco and Sun, didn't fall victim to the curse.) Odd but true—and it adds to the superstition of having the spotlight on your company, whether due to hype or not.

In 1998, Yahoo! was the recipient of this prestigious award. It looks like they might escape the pall hanging over the award; perhaps they've broken the cycle. But you can bet on a few things: their competitors are poised to capitalize upon any sign of trouble, the observers are looking (and many are hoping) for Yahoo! to stumble, and Yahoo! will have to continue its remarkable, meteoric rise just to maintain the perception that it's doing well. That's the price of hype.

Chapter 32

What about a Family Affair?

For a time, Pointcast was one of the most heralded new Internet names. The company rode a swelling wave of good press and industry buzz. Originally founded as PED, a personal software company that provided electronic publishing, it later switched focus to the Internet. Reborn as Pointcast, the company was one of the first (and certainly the most visible) to focus on the Internet phenomenon of "push"—delivering information to the desktop so the customer didn't have to spend time searching it out on the Web. It was a novel plan, and millions of consumers downloaded the Pointcast client to get their news and information delivered. Pointcast was one of the earliest Internet success stories.

But then a series of problems cropped up that threatened Pointcast's upward momentum. They began when corporate customers began complaining about the product. It seemed that when their employees downloaded the Pointcast software from the Web, a huge glut of data resulted, thanks to the way the product was architected. Like cholesterol clogging a healthy artery, it was cutting off the flow of data, effectively bringing corporate networks to a standstill. Understandably, the customers were not happy about it.

When the problem of the clogged corporate networks came up, it appeared to the outside world and to Pointcast customers that the company was taking a long time to solve the problem. In the midst of this turmoil, it was reported in the news that a large, publicly held media company was seeking to buy Pointcast for several hundred million dollars. The offer was a good one, reflecting the high hopes surrounding the company. Unfortunately, it seems that when Pointcast's sales failed to measure up to expectations—a problem due in part to the corporate network clogging problem—the acquiring company pulled its offer.

By the late 1990s Pointcast was struggling, and in 1999 it merged with a smaller private company. Unfortunately, for a company with such a promising beginning, it appears that the founders, employees, and investors realized little monetary compensation for all of their hard work and effort.

It seems that, like most start-up companies, Pointcast had a lot of issues. But according to many employees, at least one of the issues contributing to problems in decision making and management was the fact that two of the company's key senior managers (the CEO and the head of software development) were related—they were brothers. The overriding problem is one that tends to crop up anytime senior managers or founders are related, either by blood or by marriage: their objectivity tends to go out the window, and the already complicated business of growing a company becomes that much more difficult.

This is why venture capitalists are reluctant to invest in family business situations. Let's face it: none of us are very objective when it comes to family. Businesses, particularly venture capital–backed businesses, require a lot of objectivity. Decisions have to be made for the good of the company, not the good of the individual or family. When married couples, or teams of siblings, act in concert as a decision-making unit (as they usually do), it makes them a lot less open to rational argument. In the case of married founders, for example, the board is generally forced to convince both founders of a difficult point, as they tend to act as a unit. In a situation where the founders aren't related, the board can try to convince one founder of a point, thereby allowing one founder to reason with the other.

Many entrepreneurs, in fact, realize that venture capitalists are sensitive to this issue, and they put off telling investors an employee is related until well into the due diligence process. But this is a double mistake. Not only is the news of the family tie worrying, but concealing it starts the relationship off on the wrong foot.

Family affairs are stressful all around—for investors, employees, the board, and the families themselves. Think carefully before you risk your relationship with your spouse or sibling—or your brilliant idea—on going into business with family.

Chapter 33

You Can Never Be Too Rich, Too Thin, or Too Paranoid

It was the Duchess of Windsor—the former socialite Wallis Simpson—who supposedly coined the phrase, "You can never be too rich or too thin." In the circles in which she moved, those two qualities were virtual guarantors of success. In the world of start-up companies, being thin is neither here nor there—but being rich is helpful, as is another, less obvious quality: being paranoid.

Being rich is helpful for obvious reasons, but it's not something companies can typically control. Market conditions and many other factors can hinder efforts to raise money. Being paranoid about the competition, on the other hand, is within the control of every company, and it's something all of them should practice. The following example shows why.

Pete S. was the CEO of a start-up company that provided network equipment software. He was an intense, wiry guy who talked very fast and fairly vibrated with energy. Some part of Pete was always in motion. In his last job, he had been a vice president of marketing at a successful, publicly held communications software company. Now he was a first-time CEO. He knew he would need guidance, so he had recruited two CEOs from successful software companies to be on his company's board of directors. These two CEOs were in fact able to give him plenty of helpful operating advice—but despite their extensive operating experience, they, like I, failed to warn Pete to remain extra paranoid about his competition.

In the company's first full year of shipping software, things were going pretty well. We had successfully recruited a new vice president of sales and our first vice president of marketing. Sales were ramping up nicely, at nearly a million dollars a quarter. We had a number of corporate references, some of which included very high-profile *Fortune* 1000 corporations. So far so good.

Pete's company had scattered competitors of various stripes and flavors, but only one that was really a direct competitor. This competitor was also a start-up, and it had been founded around the same time as Pete's company.

Pete had scoped out his competition—including his direct competitor—fairly well. He was the kind of CEO who liked to get deeply involved in product decisions, and he could recite feature for feature the difference between our product and theirs. He believed our solution was not only different from theirs, but also superior, a point he took care to make at board meetings.

As we looked at the playing field, I began to feel relaxed about our position in relation to the competition. It wasn't so much Pete's belief in the superiority of our product that swayed me; it was that our competitor didn't seem to have made much progress—certainly not as much as our company had anyway—on getting customer installations and references. I didn't know for sure why this was the case, but the mere fact of it lulled me—and all of us—into a dangerous complacency. We continued on our path of slowly, deliberately growing sales.

You've probably guessed what happens next. In failing to sleep with one eye open, we were blindsided. Our first indication that we'd been outmaneuvered came with an announcement from our competitor: they had formed a new strategic relationship with the leading network management firm.

In a single maneuver, they had outplayed us on several fronts. Their new strategic partner was the leading company in our sector, with hundreds of large corporate customers. And now they were going to be selling our competitor's software to their installed customer base. And, for a dash of salt in our wound, the strategic partner was also committing to a $40 million investment in addition to the marketing relationship, an amount that dwarfed the paltry war chest of $15 million we had just raised.

In an instant we were transformed from complacent leader to underdog. While we had slowly been building a customer base, our competitor had, in one fell swoop, gotten access to hundreds of interested customers. And what's worse, we didn't realize how badly this would affect us until later. After all, new customers still continued to call us. Our product continued to get excellent reviews and references. But after a while we realized our sales cycle was lengthening noticeably. And it wasn't by accident.

Our competitor's large strategic partner was "fudding up" our sales—a classic strategic maneuver that larger companies use on smaller ones. "Fud" stands for creating fear, uncertainty, and doubt, a condition under which few decisions—particularly purchasing decisions—are made by customers. Here's how "fudding up" works: a large company announces a new product, and because the company already has extensive, long-term customer relationships, the customers automatically give it consideration. The trick is, the larger company may or may not actually have the product ready to sell. But because the customer is now considering the product, and because they have to wait until it comes out to see if it's really as good as the company claims, the decision cycle—and therefore the sales process—is lengthened. For a small company with small cash reserves, that can be a severe blow, which is exactly why the bigger companies (IBM and Microsoft, for example, are often accused of "fud") do it.

Our product was good, and we knew our company could usually prevail with the customer in the end. But when our sales process became longer and more difficult, we missed the plan for the quarter, as many of our projected sales ended up stretching into the next quarter.

It took us a few months to do it, but Pete did eventually respond to the new threat. We created new products and strategic marketing relationships of our own, and we made plans to raise more money. Pete and the company are recovering from this relationship. In fact, the company is stronger, more successful, and more driven than ever. But if we hadn't allowed ourselves to become so complacent in the first place—if we had viewed our competition with constant paranoia, an expectation that they could suddenly sting us like they did—we wouldn't have gotten into the underdog situation that we did.

In hindsight, Pete also realized that he should have been talking with larger technology companies, even though he felt his company was ahead of the competition. At the time, he felt it wasn't necessary, because his company wasn't involved in any of the three classic types of marketing relationships between large and small technology companies: (1) joint press releases (with no revenues involved); (2) an outright acquisition; or (3) the smaller company's utilizing the distribution channel of the larger company—typically original equipment manufacturers (OEM) agreements.

Because he wasn't interested in these options, and because the larger players in his industry were competitors, he simply chose not to talk with them. Now he feels differently. His advice is: always talk to the larger players—the "Big Boys," as he calls them—even if they are your competitors. After all, if they're not talking to you, they're probably talking with your smaller competitors. And that leaves your company open to the kind of blindsiding that initially threw us off of our stride.

I learned my lesson the hard way: in creating start-up companies, you can never be too rich or too paranoid—or too much aware of your largest competitor's current thinking.

The Fine Line

between

Bizarre and

Brilliant

The Fine Line between Bizarre and Brilliant

While we always keep business plans and entrepreneurial ideas confidential, I thought that sharing general notions about some of the more interesting plans that we've seen would be educational. In my time as a venture capitalist, I've come across some pretty odd-sounding proposals. In a job where dreams are a stock-in-trade, it helps to remember two things: First, sometimes the passage of a few years will show that a seemingly ridiculous idea was actually simply ahead of its time. And second, there's a very fine line between bizarre notions and brilliant ideas. That line fades to a blur in some of the following:

The Portable Backyard Nuclear Reactor: A few years ago an entrepreneur came to me with the notion that energy was simply not free or plentiful enough. His solution: a miniature nuclear reactor, one that could fit in the backyard of your average suburban home. And for extra convenience, he planned to make it small enough to fit snugly in the back of a truck. So not only would you always be in control of your own energy source, but you could carry it with you—a welcome sight pulling up to a neighborhood wiener roast.

The Intelligent Humanoid Robot: One company's goal was the development of a humanoid robot—intelligent, mobile, and instinctive in its behaviors. No Pollyannaish delusions among these entrepreneurs: they recognized the threat of an intelligent robot getting too smart for its own good and going out of control. So they had developed an ingenious watchdog circuit, which would monitor the robot for signs that it had somehow become aware of its status in life

Safely relegated to blissful, labor-intensive ignorance, the robots would be put to work via rental agreements—not bought or sold, as that would be tantamount to slavery. And voilá! A company could hire a hardworking, fire-resistant, intelligent employee who never required sick days, holidays, or bathroom breaks.

Digital Datawac: One business plan I received wasn't so much bizarre as it was unintelligible. Neither my associate nor I could figure out quite what the company was trying to accomplish. So turning it down was difficult: how can you turn down something you can't even understand?

Here's a sample description from the business plan:

> This is a startup business that is pioneering the technological reform of data warehousing and analytical processing into the next generation of systemization. The company's software climate eliminates the probing of redundant data for resolutions that are severely time consuming for business administrators and organizations. . . . Furthermore, this technological progression will procure the transformation of data into convenient procedural electronic automation.

Huh?

Forensic Animation: This business plan was actually quite credible and reasonable, but the underlying notion was a bit weird. The company planned to provide special animation to reenact violent crimes, to help juries visualize crime scenes better. Market size was clearly an issue here. And how in the world would an investor do due diligence on the company's product, to see whether it works or not? I envisioned us attending a murder trial, observing the jury as they watched the company's reenactment animation. . . . Guilty? Or innocent? Invest? Or pass?

The Earthworm Planting System: "Is the World Any Better Off for My Being Here?" was the subject heading of an e-mail one of my partners received from an aspiring entrepreneur. He was a farmer who had devised a method for introducing earthworms into a field as it was being planted. This is not exactly up IVP's technological alley. But we were intrigued, partly thanks to the entrepreneur's unusual level of commitment to his idea: he believed God had put him on earth for the purpose of saving earthworms.

He knew better than to think he could sell the plan to us simply through divine intervention, of course. His practical arguments were ready: the market was huge, he assured us. And he had ready references: this entrepreneur told us we could ask anyone living in the Iowa county he called home about his good character. The partner who received his e-mail was interested in obscure research ideas, but this one was a little *too* obscure.

Venture capitalists bet on dreamers because, frequently, though their dreams may seem outlandish, the only thing that separates them from possibility is lack of business experience, lack of market awareness, or simply timing. Keep in mind that some of the most influential ideas of this century were initially considered crazy dreams. Consider the following quotes:

"What use could this company make of an electrical toy?"

WESTERN UNION PRESIDENT WILLIAM ORTON, DISMISSING
THE IDEA OF PURCHASING ALEXANDER GRAHAM BELL'S
TELEPHONE COMPANY IN THE LATE NINETEENTH CENTURY

"The horse is here to stay, but the automobile is only a novelty—a fad."

A BANK PRESIDENT'S ADVICE AGAINST INVESTING IN FORD
MOTOR COMPANY IN 1903

"There is no reason for any individual to have a computer in their home."

KENNETH OLSEN, FOUNDER OF DIGITAL EQUIPMENT CORP.,
IN 1977

The Dumbest

Decision

I Ever Made

The Dumbest Decision I Ever Made

At our annual IVP partners' offsite we have a somewhat unusual tradition. At one of the dinners, we go around the table and talk about our biggest mistakes. There are plenty to choose from, of course: we've all failed to pursue opportunities that turned out to be huge and backed companies that flopped. At this dinner we have the chance to talk about our mistakes in an open, unembarrassed way.

It's a great way to get to know the partners better, to form a little tighter bond with them. Sometimes we see sides of one another we've never seen before. One thing I do remember—and won't ever forget—is one of the mistakes I described at this dinner: The dumbest decision I ever made. Here's how it happened.

Early in 1995 I reestablished contact with an old friend of mine named Jerry Kaplan. Jerry and I met back in the mid-1980s, when Alex. Brown had taken public a company he'd founded. I got to know him better during the time he was a vice president at Lotus Development, a company I followed as a securities analyst. Then my husband, David Liddle, and I were both involved in Go Corp., the pen-based computing company Jerry founded and eventually wrote a book, entitled *Startup*, about—David was a board member, and I had helped the company in its sale to another company.

So I knew Jerry pretty well. But we had been out of touch for a few years when he showed up at our offices in early 1995 with an idea and a brand-new company. Jerry was interested in retailing on the Internet. I liked Jerry and thought Internet retailing had a lot of promise, so we met several times more, discussing and honing ideas. In the course of these discussions, we talked about possibly using auction as a method of selling products over the Web. This was a great idea, I thought: not only does auction make the selling process more efficient, but it also makes it fun.

I invited Jerry to present his company to my partners, hoping they would be as enthusiastic about the idea as I was. Jerry gave a good presentation, but the reaction of the six or so partners in the room was mixed. One partner suggested Jerry get a consumer expert to assess the market, because "we know next to nothing about consumers and always lose our shirt." Another partner expressed worry about Jerry's track record—after all, Go Corp. had seemed like a sure thing, but it flopped. Another partner ventured the opinion that retailing was a tough sector for venture investment. Several of the partners were intrigued with the idea but had similar issues.

My gut feeling was that Jerry's idea was really interesting, and I knew Jerry was smart, ethical, a hard worker, and not a quitter. But what if I was wrong? I didn't want to look stupid in front of my partners. They were lukewarm to the idea, not against it: I could have gotten them to agree to the investment if I had had the courage to do so.

OnSale was one of the earliest auction services and electronic commerce opportunities on the Web—a sector that has since exploded in popularity. The partners were fairly open to the idea and it would have been the perfect time to invest. But at that time I had been a partner at IVP for less than a year. I had made one Internet investment in January 1995, and I was raring to do more. But at the same time, I was new, and I didn't feel all that secure in my investment judgment yet—particularly with Internet companies.

So I wimped out, too nervous about the consequences of possibly being wrong to seize the opportunity of being right. In venture capital, missing a good opportunity is even more painful than making a bad investment. This was a decision that I would later regret.

I called Jerry and passed on the opportunity, blaming it on the retail nature of his business. He was a little surprised, because he knew I believed in him and that I liked the idea. He hadn't factored in any expectation that I would just be afraid.

Jerry ended up getting an investment from John Doerr at Kleiner Perkins, the same venture capital firm and partner that had invested in Go Corporation. The company Jerry created—OnSale—went public the following year. OnSale, which once achieved a market capitalization of $2 billion, ultimately merged with Egghead, an online computer retailer, and was valued at approximately $400 million. The company also has recently finalized a marketing relationship with Yahoo! for auction services, is rumored to be an acquisition target by Amazon, and is well placed to take full advantage of the electronic commerce revolution.

Don't get me wrong: OnSale is not the only opportunity I've passed on that has later gone on to become successful. I helped my partners to make a "pass" decision on eToys when it was brought to us for a $50 million pre-money valuation. (eToys later went public with a value of over $7 billion.) But OnSale is the only one I passed on knowing full well I was making a mistake. In other situations, I had legitimate reasons for passing—team issues, business model issues, valuation issues, or other compelling problems. But in this case I passed for only one reason: fear of making a mistake.

I recently saw Jerry at a technology conference and took him aside to confess my reason for having passed on OnSale. In his usual understanding way, Jerry told me, "My deal was extremely risky. I understood why you passed." Jerry seems to have forgiven me, but one thing is certain: no other founder will have to worry about the same thing from me now. I learned my lesson with OnSale. I'm sure I will continue to make mistakes, but they won't be from fear of making one.

Valuation
and More

Chapter 34

You Can Have a Small Piece of a Large Pie or a Large Piece of Nothing

Determining the valuation of a company is one of the most compli-cated and arcane discussions an entrepreneur has with investors—and one of the most important. After all, the determination of valuation will affect how much of the company the entrepreneur ends up owning. It's much more art than science, and a thousand myriad factors—factors over which the entrepreneur may have little control or knowledge—enter into the decision. These include (but aren't limited to) the follow-ing issues:

- The potential return on the investment
- Recent valuations of similar type and stage investments
- How willing the investors are to pay to get in the game, if they feel they're currently out of it
- References and track record
- The perceived strength of the company's management team
- Other prior investors in the company (if there are any) and their reputations and investing history

- The potential investors' current workload
- Market valuations of similar, successful companies
- How "hot" the company's deal is (or is perceived to be) competitively

These are some of the big ones, but the list of factors influencing a valuation discussion is really endless. For a first-time entrepreneur, this dance appears pretty confusing. Still, it's better to acknowledge this than to underestimate how complex the factors are. Once, at a panel for entrepreneurs, I had an attorney ask me to calculate the valuation of one of his client companies, based only on his description of the company and the stage it was in. I had to restrain myself from chuckling, but he was deadly serious—he thought it was that easy, and he was the person advising the start-up company about valuation.

At the end of a valuation discussion, both the entrepreneur and the investor should feel like people do after a house purchase: the seller usually feels like he received too little, and the buyer usually feels like he paid too much. Sometimes the entrepreneur doesn't have the leverage to do more than take what's offered: that's okay. If this company is successful, he or she will have more leverage—in the valuation discussion—for the next company.

The most important notion to keep in mind is that the valuation is the beginning game, not the end game. The title of this chapter really spells out what an entrepreneur should be keeping an eye on. Here's the thing: In the end, if a company isn't worth much, it doesn't really matter how much of it the entrepreneur owns. He or she will make very little, and a lot of effort will have been wasted. On the other hand, if the company ends up being worth a lot, then owning even a small part usually results in tens of millions—or even billions—for the entrepreneur. So the end game is really this: You want to have a company worth a lot of money.

Entrepreneurs who have already started successful companies generally take one of two approaches to the next companies they found: (1) They believe their investor/partner played a minor role in their earlier success story, and this time they want to own a bigger percentage and do it themselves. This approach often doesn't work. The entrepreneur may think he's the real key to the success, but just as often it was a combination of factors, and he is ultimately unable to repeat the success. (2) The entrepreneur realizes that he created a winning partnership the first time around, and he wants to try it again with the same partner/investor in the hope of having the same kind of success. Whether the company ultimately succeeds or not depends on many factors—but at the very least, in utilizing the same team, the relationship among the partners is generally smooth, which can only help the process.

Entrepreneurs are well advised to line up all the elements that contribute to success—investor, money, team, technology, etc.—on their side. "Big pie" successes come from big pie thinking, and that usually means sharing the pie with the employees and investors in order to attract the very best talent.

Chapter 35

Manhattan Was Bought
for a Bunch of Beads

A few years ago a young man named Matthew R. came to us looking for an investment in his new company. Matthew had been an excellent student in a class my husband taught at Stanford, and later he had worked for my husband's company. He was a very capable developer, and he had, with a cofounder, architected and developed an impressive Web-based project manager services company. When Matthew came to us, the earliest versions of the software were complete, the company had a few early customers, and they had a little bit of revenue from consulting related to software sales.

I liked Matthew. He was a good software architect and developer. He was very quiet and thoughtful, but when he spoke about his product you could immediately sense that he had the passion required of successful entrepreneurs. He was smart, but he didn't talk about his product in a detached, academic way. Matthew also recognized his own limitations—he knew he couldn't manage a large development team. So while he worked as the company's chief technical officer (CTO), he was looking to hire a vice president of engineering.

Matthew had received his initial funding from his uncle's investment bank. The terms were a little extreme—Matthew had guaranteed a number of rights to his early investors, including a specific markup in the next round—but nothing too unusual in a family-backed, non–venture investor enterprise. Still, in order to complete any future financing we would have to restrict many of those rights. But we hoped that he and his family would be reasonable.

Like some first-time technology entrepreneurs, Matthew had erroneously believed that bringing a full team to the financing was important. As an entrepreneur, he had neither the contacts nor the knowledge to attract the very best management team; as a result, the one he had assembled was not very seasoned. We believed that we would have to help hire new managers for almost every senior management position in the company. And in addition, since the company had no CEO, we would have to help hire an interim one to run it until a full-time CEO could be recruited.

There were no venture investors currently invested in the company. This meant that we would either have to do all this work alone, or recruit another venture capitalist to invest in the company and to share part of the workload.

It was a daunting prospect, but Matthew didn't seem to grasp how much work it would take. In his view, the difficult part of building the company was almost done: they had created the software (an early release version had been tested and was almost ready), they had early customer interest and they seemed quite bullish on the product, and he expected his uncle to invest again in the current round. In addition, Matthew believed his management team was workable. So the worst-case scenario, as he saw it, was that we needed to hire a CEO and the vice president of engineering.

From our point of view, on the other hand, we needed to recruit a whole new management team and hire an interim CEO almost immediately. This is difficult enough in any area or industry, but remember, in the rarefied air of Silicon Valley it's a nightmare. Every good manager gets scores of offers, and the competition is beyond intense. In this atmosphere, recruiting for five senior management positions, plus an immediate interim CEO, was going to be a major ordeal. Yes, we were interested in investing in the company—but to tackle the huge task of recruiting, we wanted to get a pretty attractive valuation in return.

There was another hitch: we were under time pressure. I was leaving on a much anticipated two-week vacation in two days, so we needed to get back an answer fairly quickly. But Matthew and his team weren't sure they wanted to accept my offer. After all, they owned nearly all the company as things stood, and now we were asking them to give up a significant portion in order to attract new management and investors.

They asked for more time. Normally that would have been no problem. Unfortunately, we didn't really have the time to give. We were not able to go forward with the financing.

After about a year, Matthew and his team came back. They had received additional financing from Matthew's uncle, and they had continued to build software and attract customers. But they had not received any venture funding, and they still didn't have a seasoned management team. A whole year had passed and the company was facing the very same problems. A lot of precious time had been lost.

Even though Matthew's company may yet succeed, I was concerned that his and his team's bootstrap mentality—not wanting to give up something in the short term in order to build for the long term—was bound to continue to hamper it. Matthew was counting on the potential of what he was developing to have big returns for himself. But potential is worthless unless it's ultimately realized. And you need a great management team to help you realize potential.

With the help of a great management team, Matthew's company could have thrived. But because he wouldn't sell it for what seemed like only beads to him, his company might not grow like it could have, fulfilling the potential Matthew saw for it.

Chapter 36

Brother, Can You Spare a Dime?

Getting initial funding from family or friends may be a great first step in financing a start-up. And sometimes that support may be the only way to get a company off of the ground—some ideas are, after all, ones that only a mother could love. Hundreds of entrepreneurs have gone on to success after receiving their initial funding from friends, relatives, and neighbors—or even from their dentist or squash partner.

When getting funding from friends and family, there are a few key things to keep in mind.

1. *Set up the initial capital structure correctly.* Otherwise, the company will be plagued with problems throughout its life.
2. *Remember that winning big requires a great team.* And to attract that team, founders need to share the company's stock.
3. *Get advice on setting up the company's structure from professionals who specialize in exactly that.*

Setting Up the Capital Structure Correctly

There are four "buckets" of ownership to consider when setting up a company's initial capital structure. Stock must be allocated for:

1. The company's existing team, including the founders;

2. The existing investors—in this case, friends and family;
3. The company's future team (executives and employees who will be hired later); and
4. Future investors that the company will need to attract.

The size of these allocations is affected by several things: what stage the company is in, how much money the company wants to raise, and what the appropriate proportions or ratios are among these allocations.

One common mistake made in young companies is allocating too much stock to the founder or founders. This leaves too little stock for the future employees or investors. Another problem is allocating too much stock to friends-and-family investors. For example, if a founder gives his cousin Bob 70 percent of his company for $70,000, that implies a $100,000 value for the company. When it comes time to approach venture investors, they may believe that the value of your company is a lot higher, but they won't believe that Bob should own anywhere near 70 percent of it. The investors will want to put the stock in the hands of the executives, employees, and investors who will make the company successful—and that may well not be Bob.

As a general rule, the earliest investors make the most money on investments. This is because they are investing at the lowest price. But friends and family probably won't be able to commit funds for subsequent investment rounds—they're only around to get you kick-started in the beginning. So if you give your friends and family a large part of the company at a low price, and then invite venture investors later to give you continual support at higher and higher prices, that generally does not go over very well.

Venture capitalists are ready to go the long haul: we're ready to provide recruiting help, partnering expertise, and money through the rough patches. We're ready to take the enormous risks associated with seeing a company through all phases of development. In return, we require a fair amount of stock. So make sure you don't give too much away already to friends, family, or yourself before you even get to the venture capital financing.

Providing for a Great Team

Leave enough stock to hire great people. As many-times entrepreneur Warren Weiss says, "People aren't everything in the technology business; they're the only thing." So founders need to ensure they can get the best people possible.

As a rule, we venture capitalists encourage entrepreneurs to set aside 20–30 percent of their company in the employee pool—stock reserved for future executives and employees. These aren't hard-and-fast numbers. Remember, in Silicon Valley, the competition for great people is hyperintense, so founders must be prepared to offer the best packages they can.

Numbers vary depending on the company, its market, and its financing history, but these days in Silicon Valley it takes approximately 8–10 percent of a company's stock to attract a great CEO and about 2–3 percent each for the executive-level marketing and engineering positions. Because they receive commissions, executive salespeople can be hired for about half that—generally 1–1.5 percent.

I can't stress enough the importance of making sure there's adequate stock left for future employees. If founders of a company haven't done so, and they come to a venture capitalist for funding, we'll insist that they do. If most of the stock in the company has been given to the founder, the local investor, or Cousin Bob, the ratio will have to be changed, and the stock from the employee pool will come out of their portions.

Getting Advice from Professionals

For anyone starting a new company, it's hugely helpful to get advice from someone who's been down the same road—and, more importantly, from someone who's not involved in the company who can give objective advice. Many entrepreneurs make the mistake of inviting a family member to advise them objectively, when the very concept is oxymoronic. Don't make the mistake of hiring a family member as your lawyer.

"But," entrepreneurs argue, "Uncle Rich is a great attorney—the best real estate attorney in town." After all, didn't Bill Gates use his father's law firm? And it didn't seem to hurt him, did it? But remember, even though Bill's dad is a great corporate attorney, he still stepped aside and asked another attorney of his firm to represent Microsoft.

As good a lawyer as Uncle Rich may be, what an entrepreneur really needs is a good early-stage corporate attorney—and the best way to find one is to ask other entrepreneurs and venture capitalists. A good corporate attorney can help guide an entrepreneur in setting up the company's capital structure to avoid problems in future financing rounds. Many provide such advice for free, for nominal fees, or even for some stock in the company, until the company receives venture financing. Finally, the big four accounting firms offer booklets that describe the mechanics of venture investing. These are good guidelines to have.

A View
from the
Trenches

A View from the Trenches

In this book I've tried to give advice based not only on my own experiences, but also on my observations of others who are building high-tech start-up companies. As I was writing, it occurred to me that in these people—the founders, CEOs, and advisers building companies—there's a whole body of untapped knowledge and insights.

So I decided to include a chapter from them, in which they could give advice in their own words—the "view from the trenches," so to speak. I asked some of the entrepreneurs and managers the following question: In retrospect, what's the single most useful piece of advice you could have gotten when you started building your first company?

Without any prompting, most gave me comments that fell neatly into the categories of chapters laid out in this book—focusing on people, markets, money, business models, distribution, and partners. Many found it difficult to limit the advice to a single element. Here are their suggestions, in their own words:

People

As might be expected, the entrepreneurs placed enormous emphasis on the importance of building a quality team:

William Park, founder and CEO of Digital Impact, a public Internet e-marketing company, is a first-time entrepreneur:

> *Recruit for success, not for failure. You must assume that the business is going to grow rapidly and that it will take longer than expected to fill key positions. So, recruit aggressively and with an unwavering commitment to quality. If your company is successful, you will have more than enough work for everyone to do.*

William has faced the issue he talks about. His company is less than two years old and employs more than eighty people.

Rick Tinsley spent many months incubating his idea at our offices. He has experience working with large companies, including Newbridge Networks, a communications software and hardware company, and he's now the CEO of Turnstone, a soon-to-be-public network communications company. He offers a cautionary insight:

> *Choose your cofounders carefully; you will be married to them for a while, and divorce is painful and expensive.*

Dave Corbin, CEO of Silicon Light Machines, an IVP portfolio company, believes team building is harder than it looks:

> *Don't underestimate the problems you will face developing a team. . . . Creating the team and managing the various personalities will take most of a leader's time. If you believe you can focus on the technology problem at hand and the team will just form up around you, you will be very surprised when you begin to lose key people as they walk away frustrated.*
>
> *As the actual team builds, new people and new ideas are assimilated into it . . . then one day, you realize that you have your own "culture." You realize that you are getting more results from your group of ten than you ever got from a group of thirty at your old company. And you realize*

that you have stopped using "I" and "mine" and you start using "we" and "our." It is a marvelous thing.

Igor Khandros, the founder and CEO of a successful chip packaging company called FormFactor, has a beautifully simple suggestion for hiring:

Seek and hire people who are much smarter and more capable than you are.

Paul Matteucci, the CEO of HearMe (a service providing live interaction on the Internet that I wrote about in the "People" section), offered an unusual and provocative perspective on the hiring game:

The lessons I've learned could fill an entire volume, but there's one in particular that I believe is counterintuitive, controversial, and critical. Stated most purely, high IQ is overrated—especially genius-level IQ—when developing world-class executive teams.

I regularly encounter extremely bright people who can't seem to find organizational success. This condition is epidemic in Silicon Valley, where scores of brilliant people live comfortably on the fringes of their companies, or as advisers skilled at diagnosing the failures of others, but are entirely incapable of engendering their own successes.

My advice is:

- *Be relentless in evaluating both intelligence and execution track record when hiring.*
- *Be aggressive in correcting your staffing mistakes.*
- *Play to their strengths; create roles for brilliant contributors that don't require them to accomplish large organizational tasks.*
- *When you run across people who, while seemingly not brilliant, manage to get things done, reward them, promote them, and don't apologize for them. Just thank your lucky stars.*

Markets

Warren Weiss, CEO of Asera, a hot Internet start-up, says that if he could start all over again, he would tattoo a few sayings on his body, so as never to forget them. Among them:

> *Trying to swim upstream against market trends is the surest way to fail.*

Warren also notes that when he was a young man growing up in Chicago, he should have kidnapped his parents and moved them to Silicon Valley so he could have started his career here.

Kingston Duffie, the founder of two IVP-backed communications companies, says:

> *There are two things that make a successful company: supply and demand. Everything else is in the details.*
>
> *People can supply a bad product into a market with high demand. And great products can sometimes generate revenue in spite of limited demand—usually from nonrepresentative "early adopters." But both of these situations are temporary. Pick a hot market, and build a great product. Nothing else compares.*

John Hamm, CEO of Whistle, an IVP Internet company sold to IBM, says:

> *Obviously my Whistle experience (beat your head against a wall for three years until you almost go absolutely crazy) colors my advice. I think it is critical to examine your market assumptions and assign some risk factor to all the things that have to happen to create a low friction path to revenue. Market risk is the absolute BIG problem. . . . If there's a known market, with demonstrated existence and evidence of a game in play, then the task becomes winning the game (somehow) rather than hoping a game occurs in trying to cause a market. (No fun.) My two cents.*

Business Models

Dave Brown, a former CEO of Quantum, one of the leading disk drive companies, is a veteran of many start-up boards of directors:

> *The biggest mistake an entrepreneur can make is to invent a distribution channel and a new product category at the same time. Each is individually a difficult task that requires time, excellent people, and a lot of money. To do them together is a herculean task for a start-up (read: impossible). So pick a new category with an existing channel, or take an existing category into a new channel, but not both.*

Nancy Deyo is an experienced entrepreneur and first-time CEO of Purple Moon, a girls' entertainment software company:

> *You need a bulletproof business model to survive. Get board members, outside experts, or other CEOs to poke holes in your model. Have them tell you the twenty reasons it won't work and see if you can show them that it will. And don't be afraid to change everything—it may be just what you need. Before you spend your investors' money and hire a team of great people, ask yourself that million-dollar question: "Is there a valid business model here?" There are a lot of amazingly great ideas for which, unfortunately, there is no viable stand-alone business.*
>
> *Whatever your company's revenue goal is, leave yourself wiggle room to cut back if performance is short of the revenue target so that you can still deliver on the bottom line. Recognize that it will take you longer than you think, and that the holy profit grail will always, somehow, be just twelve months away.*

Venture Capital

Peter Corrao, former executive vice president of Advo Systems (a billion-dollar direct marketing company), is CEO of Cogit, an IVP Internet start-up:

Know your financial partner really well, as they are going to be your business partner too. Understand their time commitment as well as their dollar commitment. . . . Are they willing to stick it out with you? Do they have the stomach for time needed to complete your vision? Are they financially and emotionally bought into your vision?

He also adds:

Write down questions that the venture capitalists have during their research and due diligence. They're smarter than you think, and their questions of today may be your company's Achilles' heel of tomorrow.

And finally:

Know what you want for money, equity, and support before you go looking. You can't hit the target if you don't know where you're aiming!

Rick Tinsley, who remarked on the cost of "divorce" earlier, has this to say about pitching your company:

In today's market, if you end up pitching to more than five firms, either you are pitching to the wrong firms or there is a problem with the plan or team. Stop pitching and fix the problem unless you simply want the practice.

Rick's right. My experience is that if it works, it works—and if it's not working, then something's wrong with your fundamental team, market, or business model.

The Kitchen Sink (or, advice that didn't fit neatly into one category)

Dan Rudolph is the CEO of an Internet software company that helps marketing managers more effectively use their Web sites. Previously, Dan was chief operating officer at a high-flying Net company that went bankrupt. Not surprisingly, his advice to a first-time entrepreneur is:

> *Validate your product or service concept in the marketplace before you spend a lot of money ramping up your company and your team. You can get a lot done with a relatively small team and small amount of money. Hire a great marketing person to help you do this.*
>
> *Many companies get into trouble by developing and selling their product only to learn that they have missed the mark. Wasting early money leads to many unfortunate outcomes, including founders like you having to leave the company or losing control of the company. Ramping really aggressively once you have the market, team, company positioning, and sales and marketing strategy right will lead to outrageous success in the marketplace for both you and your investors.*
>
> *You want to grow in this market, but don't ramp up until you know you have the business model, team, and product right. Then you should put your foot on the gas. Staying with a nonfunctional plan or taking too much time to analyze spells failure for an Internet company.*

Dave Stamm, a veteran founder of two successful start-up companies that went public—Daisy Systems and Clarify—has become an angel investor, working with Internet start-ups to develop their business models and products:

> *Make sure you've spent a significant amount of time mapping out your best guess of what the future holds, and of how your new company will excel within that future, before you even begin to recruit your team and raise money. In particular, envision how a prospective customer will*

make a decision to purchase your product over all of the myriad alterna-
tives that customer has to spend time and money on.

Start-ups often fail because the marketing and sales costs and chan-
nels were not understood at the outset. Make sure that you are com-
pletely confident that you can make your view of the future a reality
before you commit yourself and your team.

Rick Tinsley, who clearly couldn't hold himself to the "one piece of advice" rule, says:

Take a hard look in the mirror and ask yourself what position you
should hold in the company. Better yet, ask your cofounders, your in-
vestors, and trusted friends. If you don't ask, chances are you won't find
out until it's too late if there's a problem.

In the final analysis, if you want a title more than you want wealth,
you are probably not a very good entrepreneur.

Ken Hawk, CEO of iGo, a public Internet e-commerce company for
mobile users, tells a horror story with a silver lining:

When I started my company, our original rechargeable battery supplier
claimed their products covered 95 percent of the laptop, cellular, and
camcorder markets. We placed ads in airline and computer magazines
and our phones started ringing off the hook with orders for all kinds of
mobile batteries.

Only then did we find out our supplier only covered about 20 per-
cent of the mobile market. We had to say no to eight out of every ten
callers! And to make matters worse, when the supplier was acquired
about a month later, they stopped drop shipping batteries for us, but
never told us. So we were batting two of ten, and even the two we sold
weren't getting shipped. Our customers were irate and I was ready to
give up.

But one of my original investors told me, "Hey, you've got the hardest part licked; the phones are ringing like crazy. Stop measuring your success by the number of sales, and start focusing on removing the bottlenecks. Don't give up!" I took his advice on persistence and have applied it many times since.

Gary Steele is a first-time CEO, of Portera Systems, a soon-to-be-public Internet vertical portal serving consultants:

As an entrepreneur faced with the frenetic pace of a start-up, it's easy to lose sight of what's really important. Building a successful company is not about capitalization tables, equity percentages, industry hype, venture politics, or any of the other daily distractions that can defocus an organization.

What really counts are customers—not only what they say, but how they buy and what they are willing to pay. The challenge goes beyond listening and observing, but also being willing to change based upon what you see or hear.

At the end of the day, customers drive success. And success is not about where you start, but about where you finish.

Five Short

Years to a

Revolution

Section Eleven

Five Short Years to a Revolution

"It's tough to make predictions, especially about the future."
YOGI BERRA

More than four hundred years ago a botanist named Carolus Clusius planted a few tulip bulbs in a green patch beside a university in the Netherlands. Tulips were then unknown to the Dutch, and their delicate beauty and brilliant colors attracted immediate attention. At first only scholars and gentlemen horticulturists took note, but soon word of the exotic flowers' appeal spread.

A small trade grew up among enthusiasts, with higher prices for the rarest of tulip breeds. Interest in the flowers grew steadily, and soon they became the passion of Dutch society. Demand skyrocketed, and the tulip market began to explode. Prices rose, the frenzy grew, there were simply not enough tulips to fulfill demand, and soon people began trading paper tulip futures rather than the tulips themselves. Most tulips were never even delivered. And most buyers would have been unable to afford them if they had been.

"Tulipmania" reached its zenith in the 1630s, when the Dutch government, alarmed at the unrestrained craze, stepped in to regulate the market. At last the bubble burst: The market collapsed almost immediately and tulips went back to being a coveted and highly prized flower, rather than the basis for a whole market.

The tulip market collapsed because it was artificially created and driven solely by momentum. The big question today is whether the Internet stock craze we've seen develop in the last five years faces the same fate, or whether it represents a true paradigm shift, which the stock market is only reflecting.

The similarities between "Tulipmania" and today's Internet stock craze are eerie. The Internet started out as an enthusiasts' tool too; when it was the ARPANET, few but computer scientists even knew of its existence. Venture capitalists first started paying attention to it in 1994, when the World Wide Web made it a publishing medium. Companies began sprouting up and the explosion happened.

While the stock market liked Internet companies from the beginning, the real craze began in late 1997 and early 1998. Internet stocks were being priced on futures—the future revenue stream the company could generate—just as the tulips had been. This has always been the case with stocks; value is based on future revenue growth or profitability. But the difference now is the time frame: it has stretched way out. Futures are now based on the possible revenue generated in, say, five or ten years—whereas before, the time span was only a year or two. In other words, investors expect it will take that long for these Internet companies to grow into the valuations that they have been given by this heady market.

As with the tulip craze, we too are seeing signs of government intervention. The financial markets have moved to be able to halt trading in the IPOs of some very visible Internet companies, which have had highly volatile stocks. And this is only a first step.

But where do the similarities end? It is unlikely that the government will shut down trading on these Internet stocks, but it probably will continue to try and limit some of the most egregious excesses. Will the market collapse? This is a question that has sparked innumerable editorials, articles, coffee-fueled lunchtime debates, and pundits' word wars in the last few years.

I believe it won't, and here's why: The Internet is a technology change that may come once in a lifetime. It's a new paradigm, not just a market craze like Tulipmania was. The last technology revolution that had such a sweeping effect was the personal computer revolution, which also represented a major paradigm shift. Whole new industries and hundreds of thousands of jobs were created in the PC revolution—and the Internet revolution will dwarf it.

Not only is the technological impact of this revolution enormous, but so is its social, economic, and political impact. The Internet has, for example, started to erase international borders. Despite heavy censorship in China, Internet users there can access Amazon.com to buy any type of book they want—and they are buying.

The social impact is even more profound: the Net eliminates those social boundaries automatically drawn in face-to-face or even voice-to-voice contact. Gender, social class, educational status—none of these means anything in a medium where you can pose as anyone you want. Men can experience what it's like to be a woman online, and vice versa. A classic *New Yorker* cartoon portrayed two dogs, one typing away at a computer and advising the other one: "On the Internet, nobody knows you're a dog." Further, anyone who can get online can become a publisher, with the potential for millions of readers. This has never been possible in any other medium.

The Internet is changing our lives in other ways too. Surveys show that Americans watch television an average of seven hours a day. The Net is the first mass-market medium that appears to be eating into America's television time in any significant way. Imagine the impact of having kids grow up spending their Saturday mornings conversing online with friends from all over the world rather than watching cartoons.

Economically, the Internet may have even more far-reaching effects. Today, all it takes to be a day trader is a personal computer and Net access. Gone is the monopoly of specialized brokerage services and traders. And who would ever have believed that whole new companies would be created with the notion of selling products below cost in order to get subscribers?

It's clear that the Internet represents a paradigm shift. So how is that affecting the venture business? Venture capital is now much more a "hits-driven" business, with the few winners really paying for the losers or breakeven investments. Given this environment, the partners at IVP are trying to adopt much more of a home-run mentality. This orientation probably means we're accepting a few more "zeroes," or strikeouts, on our investments, as opposed to the slow, soft landings of earlier years.

It also means that if we can't invest in the number one company in an emerging market, we probably won't invest in a second-place company. The premium on being first in any Internet market is so great that we have to go for it every single time. This means we need to pour money into our investments, to help make them number one quickly if at all possible. Being an early mover and being first is paramount for our companies.

Now how does all this affect start-up companies? It means they must focus on building fast, increasing market share, concentrating on revenue growth (as opposed to profitability), and taking big risks. Those who succeed in doing these things are rewarded. That's the pattern of successful companies—especially Internet companies—today. It's a far cry from those careful, modest, focus-on-getting-to-cash-flow-breakeven days of even our recent past. This environment has created its own dynamic. The careful, thoughtful leader will get blown away by and may lose everything to the brave neophyte who's willing to take big risks to win big. And that goes for venture capitalists as well as founders of companies.

My advice to entrepreneurs in this environment is simple: Focus on getting big fast. To do this, an entrepreneur will need to raise a lot of money in consumer markets, probably on the order of $30 to $50 million. Address large and fast-growing markets, and focus on exponential revenue growth and market share, not profitability. We're in a phase like the Oklahoma land rush: Get there early, stake out the prime territory, and keep on expanding.

Though I do believe the Internet revolution is here to stay, that's not to say the stock market will continue to climb unfettered. Stock markets rise and fall, and we may well see a twelve-to-eighteen-month period where investors fall out of love with Internet stocks. But I believe any market downturn will be temporary. As long as there's a land rush for Internet territory, being number one and getting exponential revenue growth will be disproportionately important.

In my five years as a partner at IVP, I have watched the venture investing approach change from conservative to this home-run approach. The change has been wrenching for many. Some investors are in denial, some have missed the boat completely, and others are rapidly trying to change their thinking to adjust to the new environment. As with investors, the entrepreneurs who recognize this as an opportunity and adjust accordingly will win in the end.

Appendix

A Primer on Financing and Valuation

How is a company's valuation determined? The answer to that question depends on many factors, with one of the most important being the stage it's in. New companies go through a number of stages as they mature, all of which have different financing needs and goals.

Venture Capital Finance 101: The Basic Terms

Financing: Also sometimes known as an investment, this refers to a company's receiving money from an investor or investors.

Stage: As a company moves forward toward the ultimate goal of being acquired or filing an IPO, it will pass through several stages. These include: "development" or "pre-revenue," when the company's product or service is still in development and there's no revenue yet; "revenue," when the company is bringing in money but not yet profitable; and "profitability," which means the company is taking in more money than it's spending.

Round: This refers to a company's receiving financing from an investor or investors; there are a number of different "financing rounds," which are described in detail below. The financing rounds are not directly tied to the stage the company is in—for example, a company might be getting its third round of financing while it's still in the pre-revenue stage. Or, on the other hand, a company getting its first-round financing may already be in the revenue stage.

Equity: This basically means stock. When an investor receives "equity" in a company, it means he or she has received stock.

There are a number of different financing rounds that companies go through:

Seed Stage Financing Round

This is the earliest stage—definitely pre-revenue, sometimes even pre-development—of the company, as the name implies. Usually at this point there is a founder, some portion of a management team, and the idea for the company.

A prevailing myth in Silicon Valley holds that venture capitalists with large funds won't do seed stage investing, because it requires too little money and takes too much work. But most venture capitalists, even those with very large funds, are happy to participate in a seed stage financing: last year we did about eight seed investments, ranging in size from $75,000 to about $300,000. Angel investors, friends, and family members also often invest at this stage.

The purpose of a seed is usually to flesh out the initial management team, the business model, or the concept for the company's proposed product/service. At the end of the seed, our goal is to have an initial team in place and a validated business plan. The amounts invested can vary, but they're generally less than $1 million.

Because it's so new, the company will have a very low valuation at this point—after all, there's not much to value yet beyond the idea itself. The danger when a company has a low valuation is that the founders will have to give up a bigger percentage of the company than they want to in order to get the money they need. But seed investment can be structured in a way to avoid this. Convertible debt, for example, is a common type of seed investment; it allows the company to raise several hundred thousand dollars, with the debt converted into equity (stock) when a first-round financing is completed.

Venture capitalists try to protect themselves as well in this early stage. Many require that an advance agreement be reached on first-round financing (which is the step following the seed stage), so the company doesn't simply offer the opportunity to another venture capital firm after the first one has taken the initial risk and done the hard work of pulling together a team and/or fleshing out the business model.

Sometimes companies are far enough along with their team, product, and business model to move directly to a first-round financing. This can happen when the entrepreneurs have gotten money from friends or family, or from their own personal resources, or even when they simply work at home in their spare time for free.

First-Round Financing

This round is where the true capital structure of the company is established. As I mentioned in the "Five Stages of Every Venture Capital Deal" chapter, the company will generally be divided among three owners: the founders, the future employees (the employee pool), and the investors.

These ownership portions vary based on many factors, such as the number and type of executives to be recruited, the amount of money the company is raising, and the general atmosphere for companies of the type being invested in. If, for example, the company needs to hire a completely new executive team, the employee pool has to be large enough that it has enough equity (meaning stock) to attract these new team members. The main economic incentive for joining a start-up is the promise that the stock could be worth a lot of money at some point.

The employee pool (meaning percentage of stock set aside for current and future employees) at this stage might represent 20–30 percent of the equity of the company. Each venture capital firm generally requires ownership of at least 20–30 percent of the company before agreeing to sit on the board of directors and be an active investor. And if a big recruiting effort is needed, the venture capitalists may require even more. The rest goes to the founders.

There is no hard-and-fast rule about whether to have one or two venture investors for a start-up—it usually depends on the amount of work involved (getting partnerships, helping with business models, recruiting to be done). The advantages to having two venture investors is that you automatically double the number of contacts and increase the amount of help you can get. The drawback is that working with two venture investors can get complicated, and it takes more time than if you're just working closely with one.

Amounts invested in first-round financing vary, but generally speaking they've been rising, reflecting the increased costs of creating companies and competing in today's marketplace. The amount usually varies from $2 to $8 million, but there are no hard-and-fast rules. With that money, the company is now expected to execute against the targets set in the seed stage round.

Expansion Financing Rounds

When a company reaches the expansion financing rounds, this indicates it's basically on its way. It's now getting more money to keep doing what it's doing.

There can be a number of expansion financing rounds, which are referred to by the letters of the alphabet: "Series B" is second round, for example, and "Series D" is fourth round. There are usually three to five rounds of expansion financing, though I have seen companies get up to "Series J": tenth-round financing. This is unusual, though—if the company still hasn't moved out of expansion financing after ten rounds, there's probably something wrong.

Valuations in expansion rounds are all over the map, depending on the company's track record, and investors are still keeping an eye on the employee pool at each round to make sure there's enough stock to hire future employees.

Strategic Financing Rounds

Strategic rounds involve an investor—usually a corporate investor—who has reasons for investing that are strategic, as opposed to purely financial. These rounds can occur at any time, but it's generally better if they come later, when the work to establish the company's team, product, and business model is further along.

Strategic investors are attractive for two reasons. First, they often can provide nonfinancial help to the company in its market. Here's an example: CBS invested in Sportsline, a sports Web site, but instead of investing only money, CBS traded advertising time on its television network and received equity (stock) in return. So instead of just cash, Sportsline received national exposure too, another valuable commodity. And CBS got an "in" to the new media market, which was as important to the network as whatever financial reward they might reap from their investment.

One of the drawbacks to having a strategic investor is that it forces the smaller company to choose sides—that is, in choosing one or two large companies as strategic investors, it may be making enemies of others. A small company is better off not picking sides until it's forced to do so, since it is best to keep all options open.

Finally, strategic investors generally invest a significant amount of money at a relatively high valuation. This is also attractive, but it can be a downside if the entrepreneurs make the mistake of taking a strategic round too early. The reason is this: if the company requires more money after a strategic financing round, it's unlikely that a financial investor will invest at the same price as the strategic investor did. This forces the company to do what is called a "down round."

Doing a "down round" means the valuation of the company is less than it was on the previous round—a situation that can damage both company morale and option pricing (the price of the common stock options employees receive as their primary compensation). So why can't a company just get another strategic investor following the last strategic financing round? It can, but this is very tricky, the reason being that strategic investors, as I've explained, have agendas other than just the company's financial return. So if two strategic investors are investing in one company, it can require a lot of work and maneuvering to manage those competing interests. And all at a time when you should really be focusing on what your company needs, not on what your strategic partners need.

The rule of thumb is this: If a company is going to do a strategic round, it's best to do it as a later round, not on the company's first round of financing.

Mezzanine Financing Rounds

These rounds, which typically occur when a company is perceived to be twelve to eighteen months away from an IPO, are really just a special form of expansion financing. The investor is usually a financial investor who specializes in this particular round of financing—in fact, investment banks often have groups that specialize in it. Many of these mezzanine financers have the ability to buy the stock of the company privately and then purchase at or after the IPO, which is significant because they know the company and can provide support for the stock on and after an IPO by purchasing it on the public market.

Another area that tends to confuse entrepreneurs is stock. Different kinds of stock serve different functions in the life of a company. The following explanations are meant to serve as guidelines; anyone working with a start-up should really have an in-depth discussion with an attorney to explain these concepts in detail.

Preferred Stock: This is the type of stock investors usually get. There's a good reason it's called "preferred": in the event of a liquidation or sale of the company, the owner of this stock will get his or her money back before any of the common shareholders do.

The type of preferred stock that's standard for venture capitalists is called "participating preferred." This means that an investor can get some guaranteed return (for example, two to four times what was originally put in) upon liquidation or sale of the company. The way it works is that the investor gets back the preferred amount invested before the common shareholders receive anything. Then the preferred investor and the common investor share pro rata in the returns until a prenegotiated cap is reached for the preferred investor. In return for these preferences, the investor may pay ten or more times the price of the common stock.

Common Stock: This is the type of stock owned by the founders and employees. Most will own it in the form of common stock options, which will vest over some time period, generally four years. What this means is that the employee owns options to the stock, but can't cash in on it until a certain amount of time has passed. This is to keep employees motivated to help the company succeed over some reasonable time period.

Often, employees can cash out increasing amounts of stock as time goes on, finally working up to the ability to cash out entirely after four years, but there is also something known as a "cliff" associated with options. The "cliff" dictates that an employee has to be with the company for a certain period of time— usually twelve months—before he or she can begin vesting.

If the founders have been working on their idea for a while, though, they can often negotiate to vest some portion of their stock at the close of the first round of financing. This is to compensate them for the months or years they have put in already.

Investors are very sensitive—and often very tough—about stock and vesting, because their goal is to push the founder to work hard for the company in the future. After all, common stock options cost the employee nothing at the time they're granted (unless he or she chooses to purchase vested options for tax purposes), and an employee can exercise options when there's a liquid stock for the company—that is, after the company has completed an IPO. So there's a great additional incentive for employees to push their companies toward IPOs. Not only will the company succeed, but the employees will be personally rewarded in the process.

Index